permission to dance...

The Life-Changing Guide to Releasing Self-Criticism, Letting Go of Unrealistic Comparisons and Experiencing the Power of Self-Love

gayla maxwell

Published in Australia by
The InsideOutcomes Group
PO Box 158, Jerrabomberra NSW 2619 Australia
connect@gaylamaxwell.com
www.gaylamaxwell.com

This publication is the updated version of *Permission to Dance, One Step at a Time* first published by InsideOutcomes in 2006.

First published in Australia 2006.
ISBN 978-0-9872286-4-2

The content in the new stand alone edition of the Permission Journal has been revised by Gayla Maxwell in 2020. This publication is copyright and may not be resold or reproduced in any manner (except excerpts thereof for bona fide study purposes in accordance with the Copyright Act) without prior consent of the Author and Publisher.

© 2020 Gayla Maxwell

Illustrated by Mystee Unwin
Edited by Paula Wheeler
Graphic Design by Kingwell International

National Library of Australia Cataloguing-in-Publication entry

A catalogue record for this book is available from the National Library of Australia

Maxwell, Gayla
Permission to Dance: A Life-Changing Guide to Releasing Self-Criticism, Letting Go of Unrealistic Comparisons and Experiencing the Power of Self-Love

1. Self-actualization (Psychology)
2. Self-esteem
3. Emotional intelligence
4. Relationships

ISBN 978-0-9872286-3-5 (paperback)
ISBN 978-0-9872286-1-1 (ebook)

Printed by Ingram Spark

Every effort has been made to insure this publication is free from error or omissions. No responsibility can be accepted by the Publisher, Author or any person involved in the preparation of this publication for loss occasioned to any person acting or refraining from action as a result of material in this publication.

book signing

Many people ask me if I do book signings and my immediate response to this request is, "Only if you sign the book also!" My signature on your book is, well... it's just a signature really. My commitment to supporting your process already exists in these pages and in my heart. *Your* signature on this page, however, represents your own commitment to finding true love and happiness. So my question to you is this: Will *you* please sign *my* book?

Sending you love as we dance together!   *Gayla.*

Dear Self,

As I read these pages, I remember I chose this book because it somehow spoke to me, and I listened. I commend myself for that, and I choose to make a conscious daily commitment to giving myself Permission to Dance in my own power, one step at a time.

I'm especially committed to being kind to myself as I become more aware of how I may have been sabotaging my success in the past, and look forward to embracing a new beginning.

Signed: ....   Date: ..../............/............

Country Roads take me home
to the place I belong

– John Denver

In Memory of my sister Donna Maxwell-Bagdahn...

    who's life and death taught me the importance of

    releasing ourselves from resentment;

    the freedom that comes from embracing forgiveness;

    and the gift we give ourselves

    as we greet each day with gratitude...

    even and especially if today might be our last one.

FIND OUT **WHAT'S INSIDE**

introduction   page 12

what's in the dance   14

opportunities to practice   19

the stretch before the dance   20

feel guilty or dance   21
- when are we enough
- live each day…

PART **ONE**

setting the stage   page 27

would now be a good time?   29
- you're human…enjoy it
- what's love got to do with it?

i'm not much of a guru myself   32

laughter is the great healer   34

the path of least resistance   35
- what makes us who we are?
- what are we looking for?

why learn to dance at all?   40
- finding inspiration
- why do we abandon ourselves?

conditioning, control and history   43
- true leadership
- false control
- real control
- the self witness

PART **TWO**

the process   **page 53**

practice doesn't make perfect   55

about your practical activity journal   56

the dance of heightened awareness   57

removing limitation   57

personal development is a social activity   58

interaction is how we learn   59

dancing in the dark   60

compassion is king   63

use the fall to spring back   66

love thyself   69

teacher and student, one and the same   71

your dance kit   74
    determination
    acceptance
    humor

PART **THREE**

the dance of opportunity   **page 79**

7 steps in the dance   80

the steps are easy   81

qualities of a conscious dancer   82

do I need to be perfect to find true love?   83

the law of perfect attraction   84
- the universal matchmaker
- synchronicity – as we dance with others we grow
- who are you dancing with and why
- intimate and primary relationships

dancing in pain or pleasure   90
- learning from past dances
- the shortcuts
- relationships serve our unveiling
- the myth of the soul mate
- abusive relationships
- how are you responding to your soul mates?
- finding true love

so why not dance?   107
- fear of the unknown
- fear of vulnerability
- ignorance
- fear of the dark
- pride
- resistance
- fear of change
- loss of a dance partner
- just get on with it syndrome
- the inner victim
- how is your inner victim playing with you?

the dance of opportunity – step by step   117

1. observe without judgment   119
2. check your intention   121
    - love & fear in action
3. acknowledge   130
4. take responsibility   132

5. do something different 134
   ego voice
   the nasty voice of self distruction
   a gentle voice emerges
   real change begins

6. expand awareness 145

gratitude 146
   6 hints – creating sustainable change try to feel
   grateful and bad – no can do!
   Intention, intention, intention

PART **FOUR**

things i wish i knew before   **page 151**

some things just work…others not so much 152
   laugh and the world laughs with you
   as you choose… either way you make a difference
   be aware of your thoughts
   take the easy road
   connection starts from the inside out
   the body of love

relax – meditate 164

what is meditation practice? 166

a view from the mountaintop 167

success or rest? 167

the struggle for time out 168
   need to be busy
   need for protection

what is your daily practice? 169

if you can breathe	172
the truth lies in the silence	174
8 secrets of a great dance	176
summary	181
music to dance to	188

Will You Dance with Me?

In the fullness of our unrefined and raw humanness,
will you share this dance with me?

Will you stand tall beside me in a fearful world...
together focusing on the tender voices of our hearts
learning to let go of the chaos in our heads?

Are you willing to discover what true love looks like in action
and then practice it with me,
especially on the days when devotion challenges you?

And when you forget the fullness of who you are
and what Love would do,
Are you willing to be gentle... with you, and with me
so you might know what it is to experience your own compassion
and I might learn **permission** to do the same?

Will you allow yourself consent to fall down as we dance,
and then get up with dignity, over, and over, and over again
receiving my hand as it is offered?

And yet has the pain of remaining limited
become greater than the fear of doing what it takes
to unveil the exquisite, unique gifts that lay within you?

Are you prepared to uncover the part within you that is fearless,
beautiful, luminous and unlimited by love?
And are you courageous enough to allow me the honor
of sharing your passageway to this grand discovery?

Will you dance with me this dance beyond our human flesh
So together we might release the wounds of yesterday
Embrace the promise of tomorrow
And accept with compassion and admiration
All we are in this moment?

And if you should say **"YES!"**
I will bow with gratitude to this dance of infinite love.

Let Me Explain
– Why So Honest?

In *Permission to Dance* I have purposely been extremely open about my own humanness, and how the tools I share with you have impacted my own life. I did this because I believe it is comforting to know we are not alone in our challenge to love ourselves unconditionally.

In the world we live in today, it is easy to feel alone, 'different', and maybe 'separate from the rest'; and the thing is, you are different, but in a good way! You are absolutely one of a kind unique, and that is your ultimate power. But you are not alone or different in the yearning to love and be loved.

What I know to be true is that you read a book like this to better understand your own dance, not mine. I hope I've written in a way which allows you space to open up to what is possible in your own life. The ★*Permission to Practice* complimentary activity journal has been written for exactly that purpose. It provides the day-to-day activities which reprogram the mind in ways that have you dancing to *your* tune.

As hard as I tried to disprove the old saying, "you can't love another until you love yourself", I had to succumb. It's true. Until we love ourselves, we feel separate and that is the goal of both Permission books. They are about letting go of the subconscious voices in our heads, and the advertising that blasts our screens telling us we are in some way not enough. Not worthy enough, not good enough, not perfect enough to have the right to love ourselves unconditionally.

All lies. I share my story so openly because I've proven to myself I am enough, more than enough! And I've witnessed hundreds of groups and individuals use these tools to gain the same positive outcome. So that's why so honest. The goal is to prove it to you too.

★*Permission to Practice is the book used to run the online Permission webinars.*

What's in Permission?

Permission to Dance is not another self-help book that promises to unveil the secret which will have you richer, fitter, younger and happily married in seven days.

Permission is a way of living. It is a gentle process toward greater awareness of your natural power to create the gifted life you came here to live. It is a foundation upon which to discover who you are without judgment or ridicule, taking the guilt and guru out of personal growth. The aim of this book is to remind you how to live true to what you actually knew all along:

You rocked up here for a reason, possibly (more likely) *billions* of reasons, and you have everything you need in and around you in any given moment to make the most of each and every one.

Yours is the approval you seek.

You are who you are looking for.

You are enough.

We forget. So we need reminders because there is a world out there pretty hell-bent on telling us the opposite to these truths. So we can be forgiven for forgetting!

Permission is simple, yet challenging, gentle yet confronting, playful yet powerful. In our busy chaos we make life complicated. In our quiet wisdom we find clarity, ease and joy.

The philosophies found in these pages are far from *new*. In these times of best-selling motivational books, audiobooks and seminars and the concept of *emotional intelligence* having prominence in many board rooms, most people have at least heard the idea that *within us lies our true and unlimited power*. However, examples of those who bring this true and unlimited fundamental nature into their day-to-day lives are significantly harder to find!

Subtly and not so subtly we are taught to look outside in search of some*thing* or someone to follow or to "fix" us rather than trusting and exploring the wisdom that lies within ourselves.

So how do we live as empowered beings in the midst of this chaotic human experience?

The philosophy behind Permission to Dance and the whole Permission series is about providing practical ways to release ourselves from conditioning that simply doesn't work because it is based on fear; making room for what actually does bring us authentic love and happiness and the fulfilled life we came here to live.

Most of our conditioning tells us that in order to make life work *or to fit-in* we must be nice, be good, be pretty, be handsome, *be the same as,* rather than **be you, and contribute your unique gifts to a world in great need of them!** Which then raises the question, *who is this unique YOU?*

Our real power comes from discovering who we really are, **who we are most naturally.** If we were not taught to explore our given nature from childhood, how are we supposed to know how to do it now? Think about it. From the time babies are born mothers are busily comparing—all looking to find *normality*. We look for normal weight, normal behavior, and normal eating and sleeping patterns. I remember being told there was no way my baby giggled at four weeks old. Even though when I provided the same stimuli I got the same reaction three times, it would be absolutely abnormal for a baby to giggle at four weeks old so this had to be *impossible*. Wind. Yes... wind would be normal. Like I don't know a burp or a... well... the other when I hear it!

Have you ever noticed most things considered *out of the norm* tend to be labeled impossible or just downright weird. I've been called both... often... and I'm actually okay with it.

I looked around but struggled to find where we might learn to explore our natural uniqueness. Where do we find the reminders that tell us *who we are most naturally is exactly who we need to be.* Where is it made popular to just *be* ourselves? Where is the advertisement that says it is a beautiful thing to be ever-evolving, doing what feels right rather than what is safe and popular?

Where is uniqueness being truly honored...unless of course your name is P!nk, Lady Gaga or Madonna? Now *there* are some ladies who said *I'd rather set the trend than follow it!* So what do they all have in common... apart from sporting some pretty interesting bra cups? No doubt they have just as tough a gig as the next person as they try to discover and hold onto what is true and important to them. In fact they have to do their lives quite *publically* so I'd suggest at times it's even more challenging! Yet they have all given themselves permission to be the greatest performers they can be. They have **the courage to shine**, to stand out, to be brave business women, to follow instinct and say YES to their own unique form of success and expression. By the way, I am not at all suggesting any of these women might not have other parts of their lives that may need more balance or self-acceptance—they are human after all—but clearly as performing artists these women have given themselves *complete permission*.

YOU ARE ALL THAT AND SO MUCH MORE...

Getting to this place of *Permission* wasn't easy for me. Now I couldn't settle for less. Being enough and feeling worthy, feeling good about myself and grateful for what I've been given to perfectly fulfill my own life's passions; what a blessing. Why live the other way?

I've discovered that truly knowing and loving ourselves is not just a self-indulgent luxury as we might have been sold, but in fact it is our greatest responsibility! When we're actually BEING *all that*—not faking, flaunting or *wishing*—but actually *being* all that we are with head held high, we give a whole person back to the world. We're not a broken soul who is a victim to their surrounds but a whole contributing amazing human being. I don't know but somehow that just feels so much more appealing to me!

So I share many shortcuts on this path because I have tried every avoidance trick in the book. I love a shortcut. My car GPS system, whom I affectionately call The Princess, knows too well how I feel about taking the long route. I don't care how sweet that English accent sounds when she's leading down the long road...I need the shortcut! We have a good relationship. The Princess tells me where to go...the long way, and I tell *her* where to go...pretty quickly!

I discovered the shortcut to freedom and happiness is as simple as getting to know who I am by nature and *being* her...more and more and more. Easy. Yes. Well. I mean what could be easier than just being *yourself*? Who could do that better than you?

Then I wondered, if the fastest way to experiencing a fulfilled life is as simple as getting to know and appreciate our true selves, then why isn't everyone just digging right in and finding out everything they possibly can about who really lives inside the skin they're in?

Simple answer? It's hardly made an attractive proposition.

Our advertising hardly sells it. There's no money in empowered, self-loving, independent, creative and accepting human beings. How would the beauty industries make a living? Cosmetic surgeons would go broke for goodness sake and selling war would be near impossible!

In fact my experience has been that rather than making personal awareness attractive, we overcomplicate it. I found the demands of self-discovery often lead me to feeling even more inadequate.

I couldn't do it all.

Some days I could meditate, other days not so much. Some days I felt very compassionate, loving, able to live and let live, other days not so much. I would go one step forward and feel like I was getting somewhere on this happy road to love only to come crashing down with the few steps backward, feeling like I'd learned nothing at all. Worst of all I didn't even *want* a therapist or a guru! Did that make me bad, stupid, or irreverent?

As *the queen of shortcuts* I figured there must be an easier way. And that is how *Permission* came about. Working in suicide prevention and then creating several preventative programs, I had the privilege of working with many amazing people who told me I certainly wasn't alone in needing a simpler formula for SIMPLY BEING HAPPY.

In these pages we will talk more about what I actually mean when I use the word love, and I can assure you it has little to do with an airy fairy romantic, idealistic notion. It is the Ultimate Power and it is yours any moment you choose it.

I learned many years ago that to experience more joy and love in my own life I must give myself permission to choose love more often, not least of all, love for myself and my own efforts. And to do that I needed to *practice* the act of awakening, discovering, forgiving and loving myself *in the kindest way; one step at a time.*

> Allowing anyone, even a guru to be who or what we aspire to be, would have us **striving** for peace and happiness rather than **living** in the midst of it. We would still be seeking externally for what ultimately lives within. Love lies within us and spills outward…not the other way around.

I write these words and even I hear the cliché. **You can't really love another until you love yourself.** *But clichés are interesting thing*s. They can defuse the force from some pretty powerful truths. This is one such truth. *You cannot love another until you love yourself.* In my work I hear this sentence roll off tongues regularly and yet I witness many fewer such people actually experiencing holistic self love. Not ego. Not boasting, showing off or conceit…but love. I'm talking about the kind of love that makes personal growth easy, the love that makes success a probability rather than a possibility.

What could be more natural than naturally loving you? You did when you arrived here. The world revolved around you and you knew it should! If you ask yourself only to **practice** consistently, gradually unveiling and discovering how worthy you are of love, learning more about your natural gifts, realizing your passions, doesn't that sound a lot more manageable rather than having to consistently get something right?

If we demand ourselves to be happy, confident, loving, accepting, spiritually aware individuals before we are worthy of accepting ourselves (which by the way is what I've witnessed most people doing on this path of discovery), we basically set ourselves up to fail. We're left to feel guilty, unsuccessful, or disheartened after many human tumbles that lead back into old limiting beliefs and behaviors. We all fall down. **Wisdom is found in the practice of getting back up with dignity having learned more for our efforts.**

A child learns to walk through his or her determination to stand, to move, to strengthen and to evolve in preparation for the next opportunity to grow. If we are to judge every stumble, berate every unsure step, and chastise every fall along the way, we would most certainly create in this child a fear of learning, a lack of confidence and a limited belief about what he or she is capable of.

Permission is about allowing ourselves to grow up with love and acceptance. It is about learning how to take responsibility without blame, to turn mistakes into opportunities and allow growing to be what it is...a magnificent process **...an amazing dance of discovery.**

Opportunities to Practice

Permission to Practice

Activity Journal

Wherever you see this stop icon, it represents an opportunity to practice the concept you are reading about. You can do any one or all of the listed corresponding exercises in your *Permission to Practice Activity Journal*.

While the *Permission to Practice Activity Journal* has been intentionally written in a logical order to complement this book, you may choose to re-apply and/or swap the order in which you apply them.

Both the *Activity Journal* and this book have been written to stand alone, however; if you choose to do the activities without reading the book, please understand the whole foundation and purpose of the activities are to remember more compassion with yourself as you practice.

If you choose to read the book and not do the activities, find your own way to bring the ideas into your day-to-day life because reading alone changes nothing.

The icon represents an opportunity to practice. Your intuition will guide you to where you need to be. Trust it!

A BOOK CAN ONLY DO WHAT A BOOK CAN ONLY DO

A friend of mine who is a wonderful psychologist once said to me she completely disagreed with self-help books because, "They can lead people into places that they struggle to get themselves out of." In many ways I agree with her whole-heartedly. Sometimes a book is not enough. Sometimes we need someone to hold our hand quite literally as we find the courage to go into the places we have kept hidden in fear.

The *Permission* series is in no way intended to replace other healing therapies you might be undertaking. The intention here is first and foremost to contribute to a greater awareness of how some of your beliefs might be sabotaging your ultimate happiness and how you can give yourself permission to explore who you are without guilt, self-rejection and/or barriers. You may find by embracing these concepts and practices, you feel less in need of more traditional therapy; however, I believe that awakening to the unlimited truth of our true selves and releasing old wounds can be a process, which at times may require face-to-face assistance. If any of the exercises leave you feeling ill-at-ease, sad, uncomfortable, angry, or with any other emotion at all, they have done their job. If you feel *stuck* in any of these emotions, you may need to consult a professional to assist your process of moving past the pain and into your healing. I trust you will allow yourself to be guided by your own intuition and good sense.

The Stretch Before the Dance...

One of the many amazing things I've discovered about writing a book is that an author is able to appear to have all the pieces of a puzzle together in one place, knowing each detail at once and exactly in what order they should arrange it. It's all so clear. So uncluttered.

This might appear so, and may even be the case for many authors of this kind of personal growth material, but for me uncluttered perfection isn't so much the case! I get messy sometimes. For me life is an ongoing challenge because I have chosen to live it to the absolute fullest. I usually take the road less traveled so the company can be few and far between. You might relate.

I am still practicing many of the lessons in these pages and suspect I will do so until I head over to meet my sister on the other side. I recently had someone who I had working for me as a contractor say to me she wondered how I could have written this book because, well she didn't say in exact words but it was clear the inference was I was so imperfect myself. I no longer apologize for being a work in progress. If you have chosen to read a book with this title, I suspect you're honest enough to realize you are a work in progress also. Congratulations on your courage and willingness.

As we grow, the challenges also grow, but so do the rewards, that is, if we're genuinely committed to being all we can be. We are generously and repetitiously provided the same lesson over and over until there is absolutely nothing left to learn from it. If we miss the point, even a tiny bit…BANG! There it is again. Boy do I know that to be true! I can laugh at myself and at life with great ease but I figure anyone who has decided to live in their highest possible truth should at least be blessed with one finely tuned sense of humor. I'm particularly human!

So what in heaven's name would someone like me be doing writing this book. The answer: I'm particularly human! This book is about how we continue to believe in and strive for our highest vision of what is possible in our lives even and most importantly in our darkest, challenging moments. I've had my share, and I'm dancing stronger and more fluently than ever.

Feel Guilty…or *Dance!*

Guilt in all its many subtle and not so subtle forms is the grandest controlling force in our society today. Its only job is to control; aiming to hold us ransom to the belief we are in some way *not good enough*. The *Permission* philosophy is a playful and practical foundation upon which we can practice what is not new at all; the age-old wisdoms that work every time we put them into practice. This is a course in learning to enjoy the dance of discovery so when the challenges come along to knock us on our precious butts, we can have fun dusting ourselves off and getting back up on that dance-floor. The *Permission* course is about the power of learning to forgive what probably never needed forgiveness in the first place and enjoying what is possible but often hidden behind guilt, anger, fear and our insane habit of holding onto the past.

This is not a course everyone wants to take, but if you choose to apply the lessons, it will change how you experience your life. It takes courage to allow yourself to discover and be all that you are. It requires that you walk a unique road in order to have your best possible experience of life. Not everyone will give themselves permission to be that brave.

Waking up to the fullness of who we are behind our limited beliefs should be fun; a dance. One that is even more fun when it is shared.

When Are We Enough to Simply Be Who We Are?

I asked myself more than once in the initial phases of writing this book, what did I have to offer that hasn't already been said in a million different ways by so many other more highly educated, degree lavished, conventionally accepted authors who are probably also more poetic than myself? The short answer was this…nobody else could offer me. Just like nobody else can serve *you* up on a silver platter better than you can!

In these pages I choose to share myself with openness and vulnerability because that is who I am.

And what if my sharing in this way somehow gives someone else permission to do the same? It seems to be the way. Now I embrace my childlike honesty, and I smile at those who mistake vulnerability for weakness.

So this is what I offer and it is unique to me. No Masters in psychology. No letters after my name except maybe Gayla Maxwell, **N.E V.E.R. G.I.V.E.S. U.P.**

I never quit on myself because there is so much more of myself yet to discover and the mystery unfolding is amazing to experience. Even in the difficult times and the times when I feel so much less than enough I remember this:

Behind the dark illusion

Past our own limited belief about who we are

Therein lies our true self...

A magnificent, boundless soul

Dancing in the light, Unlimited by love.

I know beyond any doubt, **if I can** give myself permission to be all that I am and appreciate the gift that is my life, **you can also!**

Live Each Day

...Like You Know it's Your Last

– Richie Sambora. From the song - The Answer

Exactly four weeks to the day after the first version of *Permission* was completed in 2005, my sister Donna was diagnosed with *cancer of the almost everything*– lungs, liver, bones and brain cancer. She was given only a few months to live, and I gave myself permission to stop work and share her journey. I spent the next two and a half years on the cancer roller coaster ride until Donna passed away on May 21st 2008. She had decided the months the doctors were offering would simply not be enough to do what she came here to do. Anyone who even made a whisper or indication she might need to prepare for her passing; would be met with the full wrath of Donna Marie... Ouch! She could pack a verbal thump when she wanted to...bless her beautiful giant soul. She was determined to see her son through his final year of high school which was two years away and she made it clear that any thought, let alone word to the contrary was not at all acceptable. My nephew was writing his final exam the day she passed away.

During the last four weeks of her life we shared almost every moment. Most were in her hospital room. Some were on the scenic grounds surrounding these walls that no doubt could share a million stories of loss and pain, triumph and love. We talked and we laughed, we cried and we made promises. Her promise to me was this: "When you smell freshly cut grass it will be me letting you know I'm watching over you." Mine to her were many. Donna dictated a list and I took notes.

In those very precious weeks, my sister and I lived each day like we knew it was our last. My big sis, frail as she became, taught me how to do that like nobody else could. Of course in theory I had long understood the importance of appreciating each moment. I had read and practiced the teachings in the bestselling book **The Power of Now** by Eckhart Tolle. **Wherever you are, be there totally.** Yet I question if I had ever *really lived completely in the moment*. I had one very memorable pajama party in a hospital room in Cologne, Germany. Our other sister Cathy was on the telephone calling from Canada, Donna there with her "good drugs" (as we came to call the morphine), and me with a mini bottle of red wine courtesy of Qantas Airways. We giggled about life and about family as only three sisters could. I stayed in that hospital room every night after that, but on *that one night* we took hold of our own power and we made it our *choice* to be there. It wasn't a hospital room that night. It was the place provided to three sisters so they might take the opportunity to giggle like children together for the last time. So we did.

One of the promises Donna asked me to make, actually let's say it as it was, it was an order from my big sis and when she decided to be, she was kind of scary! With a combination of absolute determination in her voice and the usual pain she lived with and never once complained about she said, "You make sure you use all this crap in your book!" I assumed she meant the fight one puts up when they realize their time here on earth is coming to an end; the importance of and blessed gift that is life itself and the realization of friends and family we may not be able to call on the telephone next week, or ever again. She wanted her life and her death to make a difference to others in some way. I realized how blessed I was to have the luxury of more time, more life, more opportunity to use my life to make some small difference...just because I was here, and I could.

Yet I also had a much-heightened awareness of my own mortality, the fragility and fleetingness of the human experience itself. How much time do any of us have? How are we using *this* moment?

I thought it was the morphine, the reason she had forgotten I had already finished the book. I didn't say anything. Little did I know I would let *Permission to Dance* sit in a storage shed until exactly three years and five days after her passing when someone who believed passionately in its message would submit it to a publisher unbeknown to me? Only twenty four hours after receiving the manuscript they contacted me. I had no idea who they were, nor why they were calling about *Permission to Dance*. I'd all but forgotten about it. Another eight month roller coaster was about to begin and once again the truths in these pages would revisit, remind, demand and love me into stepping up to being even stronger, more confident, and even more sure I am enough just as I am, warts and all.

So when are you enough to offer a book? When is *all that you are* enough to simply BE it? What if today was your last opportunity to dance on this earth? Would you?

After several months overseas and ensuring Donna was safe in her final resting place beside her beloved grandmother in Canada, I went back home to Australia…and I lived each day like it was my last pajama party. Within months of my return I left a fourteen year relationship no longer serving my highest purpose. And after six years of agonizing pain, chronic anemia and the sense of failure that comes along with being a teacher in the world of *you can heal it yourself,* I took Donna's big sisterly advice and gave in to having a surgery that would remove my tumor riddled uterus. Some things you can just give yourself permission to do…because life is short. And it is a gift. Why live in pain, guilt, sorrow, regret or doubt, all of which only serve to limit what is possible in our lives. I choose to live in this moment, in peace, instead.

These days I take a headache tablet if water and a head massage don't do the trick. I have a glass of red wine from time to time and yes sometimes as I'm watching a perfect sun set over the water from my blessed cottage by the sea…I even have that glass of wine alone. These days when people ask about my (what they perceive to be) life too full to be *normal,* I no longer feel ashamed but rather I feel courageous, proud and *different* in all kinds of good ways! I earn a living from every different means that inspires me and then sometimes I do it all for free. So now when people on airplanes ask me the usual *"what do you do?"* question; without apology I say, "I do what I love to do…all of it! From interior design and singing with a band or writing books, to consulting, speaking to audiences and running E!Motion Fitness retreats for artists and actors. **I give myself Permission to Dance."**

When we give ourselves permission to fall down without ridicule or judgment, permission to get back up with a smile and head held high, we grow without limitation. When we lovingly take control of our lives and allow them to be a unique expression of who we are, trusting that no matter what we are currently learning, we are enough, then we actually have a good time in the process.

When we live each day like we know it is our last, we feel the gratitude, no the *bliss* that is our delicious physical opportunity to touch, speak, see, hear, kiss, and smell freshly cut grass. While I believe *I am a spiritual being having a human experience*, I am having a *human experience* and I don't want to miss a minute.

HELP!

Many People believe that success is based on a lot of hard work.

I believe that success is based on a willingness to stuff-up with a **smile on your face,** humility in your heart **and the enthusiasm** to try over again, **and again,** and again...

No, Really... ...I'm ok...

PART **ONE**

setting the *STAGE*

There is only one **True Love**

and it is constant

It knows not darkness

As it is the light within itself.

Allow it to be in your every intention

And in this way you will discover

Your true reason for living!

PART ONE setting the stage

Would NOW be a Good Time to Give Yourself Permission to have the Life You Most Desire?

This dance of discovering our unique purpose and amazing power to create is a path which leads us directly into the arms of *true* love. I refer to the kind of love few people allow themselves to embrace. Yet, each and every soul on the planet desires more than anything to experience love without condition or reason. We reach out for something that will confirm that just as we are, we are *enough*. With all of our perceived imperfections and all of our secret fears, we are good enough and worthy of being loved. And if you think there is a shortcut in denying the fear exists at all, as the *queen of the shortcut,* I can assure you this idea is only another detour off the path. It may be cleverly disguised in the form of superiority: "Not me! I'm not afraid of anything!" Appearing to be more evolved than the rest of us mere mortals, but that superior road can actually just be another long road to more lessons. I've met many people who have perfected the craft of denying their *fear of imperfection* so well they've managed to fool themselves. There is no greater saboteur to self-love than the inability to face our fears with compassion and self-respect.

In the process of discovering my own unique dance, I have learned that behind each and every person with whom we share even a moment in time, lies a part within them that is unlimited. They have the potential to connect us to that part of ourselves that mirrors the same. We have a choice in every interaction to either *be* in that experience with them—free of judgment, embracing the opportunity to discover more about who we are—or we can be in fear, pushing them away, pointing our finger outward, and forgetting the three fingers pointing back in our own direction.

You're Human, *Enjoy it!*

Recently, I met a woman who shared a story of a time she was presenting on a stage with the Dalai Lama. After the speaking event several of them were back stage talking together, and she had mentioned to him she was not a Buddhist. She said he threw his head back, began chuckling as he's known to do, and then made some comment about *not being very Buddhist myself sometimes*! Known for his honesty, humility and humor, this comment didn't surprise me at all. To many, he is a Guru.

Certainly, he is at least a wonderful example of what love looks like when put to action: a man who practices spiritual awareness daily. He has made it his life's mission to be all he can be and to share this self with a smile, and with as many people as he possibly can. Yet, even the Dalai Lama has moments when he isn't being all that he knows he is, and all that he teaches.

He is having a human experience. We all are. I often wonder why we apologize or diminish the human experience and try so hard to get back to being only spiritual. We are human and we have arms, legs, emotion, fears and so on. Sure the truth is we are spiritual beings having a human experience but we ARE having a human experience! The best we can do is *use* our human thoughts, feelings and actions to grow these gorgeous souls! Be kind as you grow.

What's Love got to do with it?

– Tina Turner

PART ONE setting the stage

Like so many people I see in my practice, I too had spent many years of my precious life trying to find happiness, while systematically abandoning every element of my existence that confirmed I had value and worth. All the things my soul delighted in were given away to anyone who would say those magic words, "I love you."

Love was the one word I would do almost anything for, and it seemed I would hold onto my self-denial forever just to get a glimpse of approval. I spent many years in relationships, romantic and otherwise, that I now understand to be abusive or at least addictive: emotionally, mentally, and even, on rare occasion, physically. I'm quite sure I didn't realize it at the time, and I certainly wouldn't have wanted to admit to how I played out my role to absolute perfection: I played the victim, who believed she would be abandoned if she acknowledged her uniqueness. Academy Award material! I was good. I suspect any of my past dance partners who might read this (and possibly wondering if it relates to them), might consider it to be a negative description of the relationship we shared. Knowing what I know now, *addiction* is an extremely accurate word for how we coexisted in *need*. It was not their intention to hurt me, nor mine to hurt them. We did the best we could at the time. These relationships were all pieces of my own puzzle. My unveiling. I am grateful to each and every one of them for helping me to see where I was still wounded and fearful and in need of more self-love and respect.

I shied away from a passion for singing because an ex-partner would quickly make comments like, "Best you keep your day job, honey!" or, "You fancy yourself as a bit of a rock star, don't ya?" A few years after he and I had gone our separate ways, and exactly four months of deciding to follow my passion, I was singing professionally four nights a week and getting paid more money than in my day job. I guess everyone didn't agree with that man's assessment of my vocal ability!

I tolerated unacceptable treatment—all in the name of so-called love. My subconscious belief about myself was that I was not worthy of a love that would understand me and forgive my fears. *I wouldn't forgive myself!* Why would they?

Neediness, insecurity, and self-sacrificing self-doubt are hardly attractive to loving, healthy people. How many times have I heard men say, "There is nothing more sexy than a woman who knows who she is and loves herself for it." She need not be a small dress size, have the perkiest boobs, or the prettiest face in the room. Confidence and a smile are so very attractive!

True love does not say, "I love you but please change the following list of things about yourself."

> Many of us are sold a story. That story goes like this. You are loveable…when you think, feel and behave in certain ways—acceptable ways. Ways that make others feel more comfortable and yet have little to do with what might best serve your own sense of happiness and fulfillment.

I've learned that true love is sometimes hard to feel in a world that can appear to be pretty loveless! But when I go quietly within and I connect to love, it spills outward naturally into the world I experience and choose to contribute to every day. This has nothing to do with how others evaluate me and everything to do with who I am *being* and how I want to experience my life. It has nothing to do with *what* I am experiencing but rather *how* I experience it.

Some years ago I read a line in the *Conversation with God* series by Neale Donald Walsh, written as if God was in his lounge room having a casual, often humorous chat with Neale. One line has always stuck with me, and I made a decision back then that in this lifetime I wanted to live in accordance with it.

I want to experience "the grandest version of the greatest vision of who I am."

Isn't that a great line? I can't claim it but I certainly choose to embrace it. Imagine experiencing the grandest version of the greatest vision of who you are. Wow!

In doing this, I knew I'd have to learn a lot more about *self-love* and I discovered love itself is just an energy. It is a moment-by-moment choice to let go of fear and open our hearts to a majestic reality. I discovered the instant I let go, my world changed—literally. How could I choose to live any other way? Why would you?

I'm Not Much of a Guru Myself

As you might have worked out so far, I am not, and most likely never will be a guru or master of anything except of course my *own* life. It is not my mission to become a guru in anyone else's life. While I have studied human behavior most of my life, I do not believe this or any other book is the answer to all things on your journey to gaining self-awareness, love and/or happiness.

Permission to Dance and the parts of myself within its pages are intended to be a gentle reminder of the immense gift that is *your* essence especially in the times when you struggle with a limiting and possibly self-abusive ego. When we know this truth as second nature, we know a deep love and happiness unexplainable in words. This book is only one of the many ways in which you might choose to open more fully, to grow more deeply and become more consciously connected to your true self.

I used to look at some of the authors and teachers who had supported my own journey and I would think to myself, "It's all right for them. They have the missing piece to the puzzle that I wasn't given in my humble little life! I'm just more of all the *wrong* things and less of all the *right* things that they are."

The funny thing is, I have also been put on that same pedestal at times and while my cheeky little ego felt deliciously powerful up there in the early days of teaching, life has a way of keeping us in check! I was quickly knocked off the high perch if ever I got too comfortable up there! I can assure you people are very quick to remind the teacher of every word she ever taught and if she isn't walking the talk without waver, there are fingers pointing! So I enjoy my *mere mortal* status and intend keeping it that way. If you're looking for a guru to follow who lives like a saint and has all the answers, I'm afraid I shall be a terrible disappointment to you. If, on the other hand you want a reminder of the life, the love and the happiness that awaits you when you give yourself permission to be all that you are most naturally, this book was designed and written for you.

Permission to Dance and all the exercises in the *Permission to Practice Activity Journal* have been written to encourage and guide you toward a place of great *hope,* knowing you can face yourself and all your ego's games. And in your darkest place, within the most frightening idea of who you are, you can know you are still worthy of the greatest love. You are a wonderful gift, if only you knew just how much so!

Even as you fall, and in fact *because* you fall, in that very moment you are given the greatest opportunity to know you are absolutely lovable exactly as you are. In these frightening places where we act as children and need more nurturing is where the unraveling and the nurturing can begin. It is here we give ourselves *Permission* to be as we are. And if we do, we are provided the experience that leads us to greater self-acceptance and love. If we do not, we affirm our lack—and so it grows.

My wish is that we might travel together as we gain greater power and condition through practice, dancing our way to the kind of true love and clarity that lifts our spirits and gives purpose to this gift that is our lives.

You are not alone. As you gradually and gently gain greater emotional and spiritual fitness, each day becomes a mystery to unfold, each moment an opportunity to dance in greater love and peace.

Laughter is the Greatest Healer

I also want to add that this process of becoming more conscious can be filled with a great deal of laughter! In my own experience I have found the element of childish, playful joy can be terribly lacking in so many people and organizations who are striving for *enlightenment*. In fact my greatest friendships are the ones in which we find ourselves and each other enthusiastically funny as we go for the fall. It's easy to identify when someone else's ego is playing up and that can be quite funny!

Many moons ago on one very cold and gusty Canadian day, I remember my "bestest buddy" Paula and I were walking through the newly fallen snow to get to school. It was a battle to push against the wind, holding a cardboard box which formed my science project. We got to the open football field (turned accidental skating rink) where the gusts became so forceful, my science project went flying in one direction and my body went flying in the other. I came crashing down, hit my *not so* funny bone, and proceeded to butt surf in the opposite direction to the school. Once I'd composed myself I glanced up ahead and in the distance I could see Paula on her hands and knees, looking like she was crying. I could see she too was fighting with the ice and wind, but at closer glance it became clear she was bowled over with laughter. She really couldn't help herself. Slapstick was her thing!

I remember the second I had worked out Paula was actually laughing not crying, I instantly felt angry at her; believing it was my pain that was causing her great joy. But then suddenly I too found myself laughing…at her laughing, and at my pain. She wasn't laughing at *me* or the fact I had been hurt. She was laughing at the situation. It was funny! It must have looked sensational! **Life is *funny* when we choose to see the humor in it.** Pain comes and goes. Our egos are hilarious when we choose to be witnesses to them rather than be the harsh judge of them.

Not surprisingly, the pain went away almost immediately as the tears changed from crying to sharing her laughter. I chose to imagine what it might have looked like rather than choosing to sit *in* it and feel pain. I become a witness of the situation with her and rather than this being a memory that was at all painful, it is a memory of how my dear friend Paula always reminded me to laugh at life.

Paula passed away very young. I figure she'd already learned her most important lessons so she didn't need to be here for long. She made enough impact on everyone whose life she touched to last all of our lifetimes. She will forever be the person who taught me to laugh at life and see it for the playground it is. To this day, I can still hear her infectious giggle, and I smile with gratitude. I could have chosen anger. What a waste. How often might you choose anger, frustration, guilt, jealousy or any other painful emotional over simply being a witness to the situations playing out in your life?

The process of discovery need not be so serious that we end up looking into every little hint of movement in our world and then analyze it to the point of missing the point! I have known many journeymen and women including me, who have been so keen to *awaken to the truth* we forgot to enjoy the dance along the way—and call me a kid, but I figure that's a big part of what we're supposed to be doing here. I'm all for enjoying the ride as we experience it!

Permission is for those who would like to experience themselves less seriously and more intimately. The kind of intimacy that makes healthy and happy relationships—first starting with the relationship we have with ourselves. Few of us were given this kind of training. I have gained much of my training the absolute longest way. Now I prefer the easy road, using the skills I have acquired along the way which allow me to experience fully the ups and downs of life's experiences while moving more gently and kindly with myself and others.

I hope Permission provides you with some shortcuts on the road to your own higher happiness. On the other hand, you may also choose the longer winding road. There is no judgment on the way you travel through your life and if anything, I would hope you will do it your way. My way is just that. Your way is unique also. As always we take what fits us at this time and should feel free to let go of the rest. You may call on it at a later date. You may find alternatives. For now, you're here. Have fun!

Following the Path of Least Resistance

I once asked a dear friend of mine how things were going in his life and I got his usual and heartfelt response, "It couldn't be better." But this time it was followed by, "I'm following the path of my heart rather than the path of convenience."

His words resonated down to my core. Just imagine following the path of our hearts rather than the path of convenience. I wonder what the world would look like if we all did that!

As we give ourselves Permission we can gently become more aware of what we're doing that works for us and what doesn't work without having to feel guilty for past "mistakes". As we do this we gradually eliminate some of the things that limit us from following the path of our heart. We learn why the path of convenience might seem a whole lot easier to take—even though it often has little to do with who we really are by nature.

Through my bruised knees and my unquenchable desire to love and understand myself, and the world around me I've learned that we are all dancing one dance or another. If we do not choose the path of our heart and dance in accordance with our own unique rhythm, then there will be a dance provided for us that has little to do with who we really are by nature.

It might appear the path of convenience is the path of least resistance, though very often nothing could be further from the truth. Life has a wonderful way of keeping us true to ourselves, and it most certainly isn't by making things easy as we take our detours! (I have lots of firsthand experience on that topic.) Obstacles we call *problems* are the universal language for "get your butt back on your own path!" They are not problems at all but rather loving messages of permission to behold our greatest visions and to do the things that bring us joy, peace and happiness.

What Makes Us Who We Are?

I think the need to know who we are and what we are doing here is at some level important to most people. Some of us make it a conscious lifetime mission while others are completely unaware of how or where to begin so they let sleeping dogs lie so to speak. Social conditioning can make the search for these answers quite challenging. Our social environment would have us believe that who we are is found in such things as what we do, what we wear and who we know.

As we reach outward for what is fundamentally an inward journey, we confuse our natural sense of worth and value with a *comparative mentality*. We try to be as good as, as smart as, more talented than, better looking than, and so on. As we compare what is essentially incomparable, we will always come up short handed. I will never be as good at being you as you are, and vice versa. For many reasons, mostly based on conditioning, we are not satisfied with just being the best self we can be. Yet I have had it proven to me many times over that the truth of the matter is this:

Discovering and being my true self is the only way to **know** the joy of living.

PART ONE setting the stage

Who Am I?

During my own personal process of unveiling my true-self I systematically went through every relationship I was having at the time, even relationships from the past, and I asked myself, "Is this who I am?"

I looked at the relationship I was having with myself and I asked, "Is this who I am?"

Now that I am starting to hit the other side of that hill we all seem so fixated on, and being one of the courageous few who are unwilling to use injected toxins to hold onto thirty-two forever, the big green eyes and healthy thick blonde hair I had taken for granted are clearly starting to change (translation: fall out! NO, not my eyes, my hair!), and everything seems to be a little less glossy and at least a few inches closer to the ground than they had been only a few years ago. The lines around my mouth were becoming more pronounced; and did you know your ears and nose never stop growing though the rest of you shrinks? (Just by the way, I'd like to know who was responsible for that little glitch in design!)

It has become too clear (even without those much needed reading glasses) I could no longer identify myself as my physical appearance, as it too is ever changing and hardly dependable.

When I was asking this important question of who I am, the jobs that used to provide me with a rather glamorous identity of both a singer by night and a public relations manager for a television station by day no longer existed. I had spent years of my life struggling to find true love inside myself to make my own intimate relationships work and with all the love in the world they didn't end with a bride and groom living happily ever after. At the same time I was studying and working as a master trainer in suicide prevention, often providing my services free of charge to charitable organizations and the financially disadvantaged. It was quite a humbling experience to go from two job titles that were always greeted with respect and interest, to watching people's faces shy away as you mention the word suicide and earning almost no money at all.

So, was I a life saver (no pun on the candy), a counselor, a charity worker, a *do-gooder* as I was referred to more than once? Was that who I was?

In fact, I realized *I* was not any of my relationships or my state of health, my clothes size, my address or my job descriptions because all of these things kept changing. I had to look elsewhere for my true identity because all of the things I had identified myself with previously seemed to be slipping through my fingers and were being replaced with a sense of *self* that far exceeded an understanding of what I do or who I associate with.

Since I can remember I had always travelled a pretty conscious road, but let's be honest here, the process of *really* letting go and trusting life will all be good in the end isn't an easy one for most of us mere mortals! In some places we might be great at going with the flow, yet other parts of our lives...not so much.

It is incredible how the world gives us plenty of opportunities to learn the lessons. Yet sometimes we need a brick to hit us on the head before we get it.

Everything changed quite suddenly when my sister passed away. *Clearing* was the order of the day, after day, after day, after month, after month, after month...I wondered how much more I could handle. Nothing seemed to be as it had been. No marriage, no children around to mother anymore. One of my big sisters, no longer there to chat to on the phone for hours and ask what comes next. I was stripped naked, bare of anything I could identify with. I stood humbly in the mirror, and even without those old lady glasses I could see the *bits* were all definitely a little closer to the ground than I had remembered!

Through centuries of conditioning, we have been led to believe we are the external happenings, the dramas, the people, places and the goings on in our lives. We're told we are the skin that is wrapped around our bones and we are the clothes size that fits around that skin. We believe we are the number of years we have lived on earth and the number of marriages it takes us to learn what we came here to learn about ourselves in deepest love and fear. We are told we are the job that we do and how much money that job earns us which tells us how good or bad we are as *providers*. We ARE none of these things. We are so much more. And our task is to discover this unlimited blessed self and take our perfect place in this gift that is planet earth! Sounds so easy right? For me it is... and it isn't. So I just keep practicing.

I have discovered that as long as we identify ourselves as the external part of the *self*, we will never know what it is to be truly happy and at peace in our own blessed lives.

Give yourself a break...

If you feel ready, now might be a good time to take a break and consider the exercises in your *Permission to Practice* Activity Journal.

Some relevant exercises to look at include:

Ex 1a   **My Family**

Ex 8a-g   **You're Not Normal—You're Unique**

Ex 13a-d **Who Do You Think You Are?**

PART ONE setting the stage

What Are We Looking For?

What is this unconscious and often desperate search for happiness that leaves most people reaching to external sources and grasping with both hands?

Aldus Huxley, author of *Perennial Philosophy,* wrote there were two beliefs that all societies have shared since the first civilizations:

- there exists something else apart from that which is changing (i.e., the physical world)

- and we are part of that unchanging something. Some call it God. Some call it Krishna, Love, the Universe, Spirit, Buddha but whatever the name, we have believed in its existence

The Only True Security Lies in Knowing Our Internal Witness

What part of you is the same this year as it was last year and the year before and as far back as you can remember? It is that part within that connects you to conscious living, the part that knows what feels right and what doesn't. As you reach in to *that* place you know who you are. Your body changes, but inside your body is a witness who is beyond the external events and dramas in our world.

That part within speaks to us through our passions, our deepest desires, our moments of greatest joy, sorrow, our hopes and our dreams.

I looked inside myself to find this witness and discovered it held the secret to my greatest desires, my boundaries, my deepest and purest potential and it held the truth about who I am. I check in with her every day through meditation.

I believe meditation comes in many forms because life and the people experiencing it come in many forms. I love to dance...so I dance with the intention of being completely present and spiritually alive in the moment. I do Tai Chi because for me that's my morning dance and meditation tied up into one. Sometimes I add Yoga to the mix because it feels right for me and what my body needs on that day. I mold clay because I love the analogy of molding my own day, my life. Some days I do only five minutes of these many forms of meditation. Some days I feel like doing an hour or a whole day. I commit to what I can or want to on that day without apology but I do commit every day to something that brings me back to this part of myself that is the *witness*. I do this not because a guru told me I had to do it in order to be good in some way or to get some magic result. I do it because when I don't, I forget who I am and I start believing I am so much less—as the external world would have it. We are more easily controlled by external happenings when we do not take control ourselves!

Why Learn to Dance with *Love* at All?

Have you ever had a moment, a day, or maybe even a week, a month or a year when you wondered what the heck it's all for anyway? Why even bother spending all this time learning how to be in loving relationship with ourselves and others? I had a client summarize her search like this, "We spend a lifetime getting to know who we are, and then just when we're getting close to actually liking who that is, it's all over!"

I say why not dance *now!* The sooner you discover what brings you *true* love and happiness the sooner you can get on with living it! You can choose to like who you are today.

I am aware this process of growing up rather than just growing old can feel like hard work sometimes. Living a more conscious life can be frustrating and on the tough days when it seems the rest of the world is getting by just by being selfish, mean, greedy and generally out for themselves, why should you bother to find this higher, happier, conscious self at all?

For me the answer to this question of why bother is yet another simple question: "What is the other option?" The opposite of dancing in love, is a dance of fear…and that just doesn't seem like a great way to spend a whole lifetime to me! If we are to be truly happy, we must learn all we can about who we are because if we don't, we end up in fear by default. We have so much fearful training around us that we become quietly and subtly engaged in a dance of pain, victim-hood, anger, resentment, inadequacy, and limitation, which are all by-products of fear.

So many people spend an entire lifetime living someone else's idea of what their life should be. Some people even believe this is enough for them and the effort to claim their life as their own seems almost impossible to achieve.

Wayne Dyer puts it beautifully in his book called *10 Secrets for Success and Inner Peace* when he says: "Don't die with your music still in you…and too many people do." He goes on to say, "When you show up here, your work shows up with you. It is placed in your heart and too often we ignore it in the name of fulfilling a destiny that has been laid out for us by other people."

PART ONE setting the stage

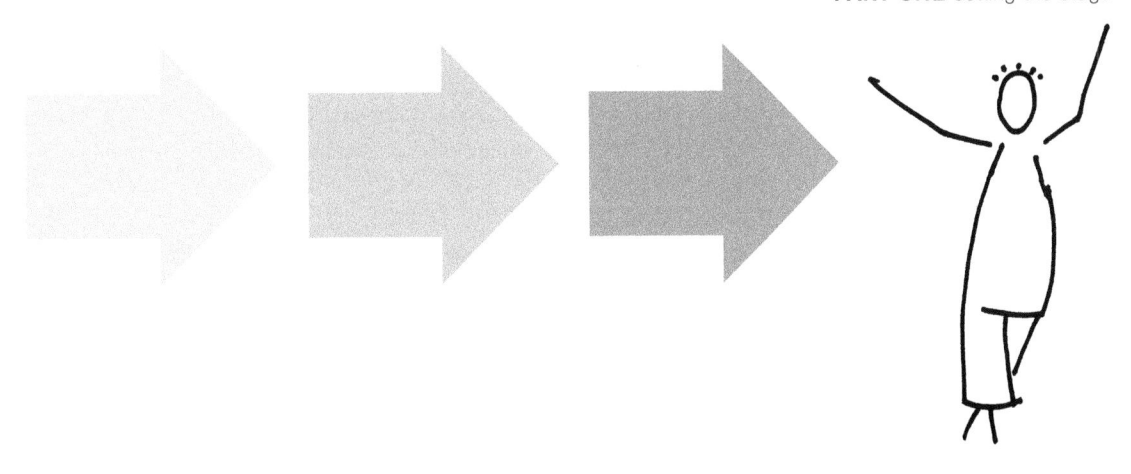

Finding *Inspiration*

The word *inspiration* comes from the same root as *respiration*. To inspire has a number of definitions related to breathing, creativity, influence and aliveness. What we are all seeking is inspiration—to feel alive, energized, engaged in meaningful creative activity.

For many years of my life I'd believed I was quite a lazy person who took the short-cut if one was available. (We've discussed the Princess GPS so we know that latter part is still true about my nature; however, I no longer judge a shortcut as a shortcoming.) There are times when the shortcut can be the best way. Why take the long road unless I really want to explore the scenery?

I know I'm certainly not lazy, I was just uninspired, or put another way, not connected to the breath of passion in my own life.

In that place of being a witness of our own lives, each of us knows what inspires us, though most spend so little time *in-spirit* (inspired) they believe they do not know. It is in this place of connection with our self—our true-self that we remember what we are doing here. Meditation serves me well in supporting this connection.

I know nothing inspires me more than communicating this story of connection and hope in every form of communication available to us. If I am not able to do that, I actually feel quite stifled. Within each of us there is something we must do, and when we do not, we feel incomplete. We feel incomplete only because we are not using our natural gifts.

If we are to know true love, a deep happiness and unlimited joy, we must find the place within ourselves that understands we are far greater than the number of candles on our birthday cake, the wrinkles we do or do not possess, (and if you don't have them currently, you certainly will—if you're lucky!) and any other changing, evolving aspect of our external world. This is *not* who we are.

Who we are is *unique*. We are full of potential and unlimited desire to know love in its purest form. We are all born with a dance inside of us, but too few people allow themselves to experience the process by which we discover it.

Ex 17a	**Candle Meditation**
Ex 13a-d	**Who Do You Think You Are!?**
Ex 12a-c	**Finding Joy**
Ex 15a	**Personal Business Plan**

Why Do We Abandon Our True Selves?

If each of us is born with a very specific dance inside of us, then why is it so few people actually choose to follow the part within that knows better than anyone what is right for them? Why do so many people conform and live the life someone else, a mother, a boss, a wife or a society has created for them?

It was obvious to me this dance or gift that is unique to each individual is the most wonderful contribution they can provide to the world. Why have we abandoned our own natural ability to give of our greatest gifts?

PART ONE setting the stage

Control, Conditioning and History

> **Our lives begin to end the day we become silent about the things that matter.**
>
> *– Dr. Martin Luther King*

I have noted that in so many ways within our own human history we have been taught that to be *the same as the rest* is a good thing, but being *empowered* and *unique* causes trouble, chaos and pain.

Dr. Martin Luther King spoke out about the human right of equality for all nations regardless of color or religion. He was assassinated. Christ who taught that the true holder of all power was not men, but love. He was publically crucified.

We could all gain by hearing more stories that tell of the up side, the mystery and the authentic power we will know as we find the courage to stand tall, and to be right with our own spirit. The fascinating mysteries and the humorous synchronicities are all a part of the experience of these men and woman who choose the path of their heart rather than the path of least resistance. Yet the benefits of choosing this path are rarely the slant put on the story. We are instead reminded of the pain, the tragedy and the question of why a spiritual life is a frightening one in which we are somehow made to take risks we don't really want to take. Certainly in my experience, living life in connection with my spirit need not be a constant and painful sacrifice. I think my life is sensational!

Governments, newspapers, advertisers, music videos, colleagues, parents and friends alike all subtly (and some not so), remind us that to fit in is more important than to be who we are.

I find the irony in this concept is that if only we were all *being* who we naturally *are,* we would fit in completely and with absolute awesome perfection rather than fighting fearfully with our own feelings of lack.

The belief we need to control our physical world takes us away from our spiritual connection and in fact collectively creates a society that is literally *out of control*. True control is *not* found in following the masses but rather in following our spirit.

True Leaders

I have observed how we are subconsciously conditioned in the idea that we must be controlled in order to be good. In other words, we collectively believe that without something or someone to follow, be it the direction of governments, religion or the direction of fashion, we would all be completely lost. We've even made God a "He" who lives outside of us so we can shunt the responsibility for everything from lack of rain to children starving in Africa. Never mind what we're individually and collectively doing to the planet to cause changes in the weather. Never mind that we have enough food to feed the entire world many times over. We say that God has things in control and we can suppose it must be *His will*. Right? We can feel safe knowing a really wise, strong, smart *guy* is leading the way.

It's not *our* responsibility! We can't help the state of the world! Yet what if God resides in all forms within and around us? What if we are a part of God and God a part of each and every one of us? Not just metaphorically, but literally. Who do we follow then?

How many of us are seeking to be led by God (love) within us? How many are *truly committed* to learning how to behave as love would behave? In fact we're told this is impossible! I am reminded with some regularity that I strive too high and ask too much of myself. I'm told that "Only Jesus Christ himself could know love as I want to know love!" But why? Why can't we be as completely committed to finding truth, love and compassion in every moment as Jesus was? I didn't read the part in the Bible or any other history book that said Jesus was given particular tools we don't have access to. In fact he kept saying, "All I do you can do also and more..." But when I raise that comment in some religious worlds all anyone can come up with is, "Yes but he was the Son of God!" If I use biblical language to respond to that, would I not be correct in saying that *I am also a child of God?* Aren't you?

Jesus was put through more pain than most of us. He faced great amounts of ridicule, hate, jealousy and cruelty—yet he chose love. Not because he had some extra mystical powers to do so, but because he chose love. And within that love, is the ultimate power to heal. Love is within the reach of each and every one of us, every moment. Regardless of whether you believe in God, Jesus, Buddha, Mother Earth or nothing at all, the power of love is undeniable, and I believe that is the message they have all tried to demonstrate to us, over and over again.

PART ONE setting the stage

We are created in

Love

and controlled in **FEAR**

False Control

We can become so stuck in the detail of our physical rights and wrongs, from wars that never end to the fashion statements that qualify for *the best and worst dressed* entry in the weekly magazines. I hear women regularly making statements about something as benign as a dress that's *Just wrong! Didn't she look in the mirror this morning?* And I'm not referring to teenagers here—grown women deciding what is right or wrong for another human being—according to the law of the *fashion police*. I say, WHO CARES? Obviously, many people care—and so we create that which is deemed to be of value, based on what society considers important at the time.

The fashion designers, editors, and advertisers know that if you are led to believe (through enough constant bombardment) that one way to dress is *right* and the other *wrong,* you are controllable! And so, fashion designers are among some of the leaders in our world at this time.

This is not to pick on the fashion industry specifically; in fact I can be a bit of a clothes-horse myself at times. I especially love the art of getting dressed in ways that make me feel unique. The example simply makes the point that we are being conditioned every day in so many ways to believe we need to be controlled by the external world or else we wouldn't know what to do and we certainly couldn't feel good about ourselves. Rubbish!

I wonder what would happen if we were equally bombarded with billboards that read: You are Amazing—Thank you for contributing who you are to this planet today!

When I contacted the deputy editor of a popular weekly magazine to advise her of my concern about a particular article with a sensationalized headline relating to anorexia, I very politely asked why we consistently see this kind of material about weight gain and weight loss in Hollywood. Her answer was quite simply, "It sells magazines." She then laughed, as if pointing to the ridiculousness of my question. We went on to discuss the epidemic of low self-esteem in young people—women in particular. (All right, it was *me* who went on to discuss it—she listened. Or more correctly, she allowed me to speak.) Knowing full well how her articles support negative conditioning, I asked her how does she, a woman (very likely to be in the 98% of women who are dissatisfied with their bodies), feel about contributing to this collective low self-image—which of course in the end, affects her also? Her answer, "That's what people want."

Real Control

I've contacted television stations about the ratio of murder and explicit sex scenes visible on television as compared to family and/or uplifting entertainment. I have waited on radio hold lines to let DJs know that competitions, which humiliate and devastate young hopeful singers live-to-air (just for laughs), is simply not okay with me. I've written to the editor of newspapers and magazines to ask why we always need to be told the ugly side of every story, and I've contacted underwear advertisers to let them know I am offended by almost naked adolescent girls dancing around provocatively and yet innocently playing with butterflies. The bottom line, (pardon the pun), is that all my calls result in the same feedback. They all say, "It sells." Ratings go up and the newspapers and underwear sell better with more *edge*.

"That's what people want," they say. And do you know how they know that? They know because complaints like mine are few and sales are up. We buy, we watch and we support their products. A handful of us let them know otherwise. Not enough of us yet to affect their bottom line. When it is enough, they will change.

Clearly this *is* what we want. Murder, sex, scandal, "reality" TV (whose reality I'm not sure), deception, glamour, hate, young girls being viewed sexually by men old enough to be their grandfathers, prejudice. For the most part, society wants to find and exploit the lowest level of ego energy in our fellow man so we might feel better about the ordinary lives we are creating as individuals. "That's what people want." *You* are people. You vote with your actions. Your apathy is the same as a vote in favor. What we're currently voting for is what we're currently getting.

This way of creating our society and what we stand for—led by our external world rather than our internal wisdom—allows us to falsely pass blame and judgment toward politicians, media, marketing and the masses as we each individually give our own power away to the outside world. They are just giving us what we say we want. If we don't speak up, we get whatever we are given.

> **None of us are victims to our environment—**
> **we are participants—silent or active.**

Taking real control is about making a choice to turn the TV off when it destroys your sense of peace, or not buying the magazine, the underwear or the pair of shoes that were manufactured or advertised in a way that no longer feels right for you or your children. There are a multitude of arguments surrounding this topic and I am fully aware of the controversial tone of the statements I am making—especially given I cannot go into the fullness of my meaning in this book. You don't have to agree with my view, but I hope this will at least open the gate for more discussions surrounding personal power at our dinner parties, our office lunch rooms, at home and within ourselves.

Internal Control is Acting on the Voice of Spirit

In closing this idea of external versus internal and real control, I want to add I am not suggesting everyone must be passionate about the same things as I am and/or everything all at once. In fact our differences create necessary balance. The point here is not to dictate to you what you should or should not do, buy, feel or think because I don't know that. Only *you* can know that. The point is **you have significant power to contribute** to the formulation of our society's collective moral, emotional, industrial, environmental and political standing.

The world is just giving us what we say we want. You have this power to co-create a healthier society through giving time and voice to your spirit. In this place of greater awareness you discover what feels right **for you.** As we listen to spirit, the things we feel are important will evolve, develop and grow. You need not be all things at once, super human healing the world in a single bound. But everyone can find at least one thing their spirit is calling them to do today, in this moment, this second, and to act on it.

And that I believe will be enough. Enough to raise the consciousness level from our current state of fear- driven chaos to a love channeled unity.

From this Place of

Giving-In to Our Core Self

or Our Soul Self

—Our Dance Begins

The Witness

With this idea in mind, I searched myself for where I felt the need to *falsely* control in my own life, and in these places I discovered what was blocking me from being at peace in my own world. I saw what was, in fact, *out of control* and what needed more of my spirit's gentle reminders of who I really am. Past my personality, my ego and my mind chatter, I find *who I am beyond doubt*.

PART ONE setting the stage

I found that self-love—and all the authentic love that follows from it originates in giving-in to the part within ourselves that is always solid, grounded and wise. This is our spirit, and it is our only chance if we are ever to be able to answer the two most important questions we can ask ourselves:

1. **Who am I?**

2. **What do I *really* want?**

I have observed, shared with and counseled uncountable people in my life and I have become very much aware of how few people can honestly answer these two questions. I am not asking the question, "Who are you *today?*" I'm asking, "Who are you today, yesterday, the day before, when you were born and ten years from now?"

I'm not asking, "What do you want this minute?" I'm asking, "What is it that you desire *at your core?*" It will be the same thing you have desired to be, do, experience and/or know since you were born, and if you don't unleash this part within, you know you will most certainly have regrets on your death bed. You might have no idea what the answers are right now, that doesn't matter. What matters is the choice you make to step towards that discovery or the choice to ignore it. In these two answers lies your hope and commitment in times of challenge.

As we acquaint ourselves with the part within us that is the *observer* of our own lives, the essence, the non-judging, the interested *spectator,* **we discover who we truly are**. We discover what we truly desire and we are naturally inspired. As the observer, we naturally find ourselves judging others less and becoming witness to their lives also, because we cease needing someone to be right and the other to be wrong. We don't need to be better than, as good as, or compared in any way because we are simply observing rather than judging what we see, hear and feel. When we become more of a witness and less of a judge and jury, we see transformation in every relationship we experience, not least of all, the relationship we are having with with ourselves. You want real love and deeply founded happiness in your life? Try this little idea on for size!

If you would like to become a better observer in your own life so you are more clear on who you are and what you truly desire, these exercises are good ones to play with:

Ex 2a-e   **Observation vs. Judgment**

Ex 8a-g   **You're Not Normal, You're Unique**

One Step at a Time...but keep on dancing!

I realized also that in order to find that place which is our true-self, very often we needed a little extra guidance to see past the way the ego tries to trick us into believing we are limited or in some way damaged goods. We have most certainly received a substantial amount of guidance to lead us to the belief we are something that we are not! Collectively we teach and we believe that we are something less, something wounded and we are in need of repair. This information is reinforced daily. If we are to own our authentic power we need to learn and practice the skills of reconnecting to the truth about who we *really* are and how to find that which is *true* love.

*This is where the **Permission** part of the **Dance** comes in.*

For most people the hardest part of learning any new skill is the part where they must confront their so called "imperfection." Once again this idea of imperfection and getting things wrong is based upon conditioning that states there is a nasty thing on earth that we have called "failure" and that is a place that you really do not want to go!

"Genius is one percent *inspiration* and ninety-nine percent **perspiration!**"

– Thomas Edison

PART ONE setting the stage

Thomas Edison was able to invent the light bulb because he had no concept whatsoever of the word *failure* in his vocabulary. When he was interviewed one day he was asked the question, "How are you feeling right now about failing thousands of times with this thing called electricity?" The man went on to ask, "What keeps you going?" Thomas Edison answered,

"I haven't failed! I have now discovered thousands of ways that a light bulb will not work!"

Mr. Edison clearly understood that every moment and every creation is an opportunity to learn. He understood it was that very way of thinking that kept him going; and I don't know about you but I'm pretty grateful for that. Without Mr. Edison's attitude we might all still be left in the dark!

If we are to give ourselves permission to dance our own unique dance within each relationship and opportunity presented in our lives, we must allow ourselves to *practice* and discover the results of our efforts without a constant back chatter about how we are somehow failing if we don't get our desired outcome every time.

For many, this concept of failure is so ingrained in the psyche it will be a challenge at first to think differently. On the other hand, as we become more and more familiar with being an observer of our life rather than the judge and jury, we begin to enjoy the freedom of discovery. And in joy we unravel the key to our natural contribution.

So, let's dance with great respect for our choice to move forward, regardless of how many times we fall down.

Let's dance like nobody's watching!

PART **TWO**

the **PROCESS**

I am in the process of recognizing my perfect design

I am enough... exactly as I am today

I am the darkness and light that shadows or illuminates my own truth
I am the Ego and the Spirit that ridicules or enlightens
I Am the Weakness and the Strength that cowers or conquers
I Am the Fear and the Love that festers or heals

I Am all that I Am . . .

and that is more than enough to experience complete and unconditional love

This is my choice

Practice Doesn't *Make* Perfect…
It *Proves* it was there all along

I must have read hundreds of self-development and spiritual books and each of them seemed to be telling me that if only I followed these five or ten simple steps, I would have all that I wanted in my life. I would love myself, and the rest of the world. I'd have peace within my soul and of course bring peace to the earth. I would know I am loved even when a partner refused to respect one of my boundaries or my daughter's apparent fear of putting dishes in the dishwasher would make me smile. I would also be successful, and I would know exactly what I wanted to do to get me there. I would be thinner, I'd eat right, heal my emotions, have abundance and unlimited power, and naturally I would have more fun in my life than I could possibly handle. Wow! Sounds great! But it never happened by the end of the book.

Through no fault of the many authors who have provided me, and millions of others with a wealth of information on this trip to living a more conscious existence, I could never quite achieve what I thought I was supposed to achieve. Oh sure, I might take a few ideas and apply them for a little while but the underlying message was clear. My ego would state clearly, "You're not the same as other people. You have no discipline, you're weak and you will never be truly happy." So once again, I was reminded I was in some way flawed. A failure. Below average. A misfit.

For this reason I want to say to you again right now, *reading* this book will not fill every gap between where you are now and where you want to be. Is there such a magical book where reading is the only effort involved in order to change our lives? Even my favorite book, *A Course in Miracles,* asks me to practice every day. Every day. Not every other day. And it insists that I only practice a little. Now that's my kind of practice. I feel teased into wanting to practice more so I sneak it in! Getting where you want to be can only be found through the *act of practicing,* not only such ideas as the exercises found in these pages, but just as importantly, seeing what it looks like to be compassionate with yourself and with others in the process, over and over and over again.

About Your Permission to Practice Activity Journal

There are so many different ways in which to practice and experience our spiritual or true-selves. I wrote the *Permission to Practice Activity Journal* initially because I used the activities daily in my work so I simply wanted to have these ideas all in one place for my clients. The most common question I get asked overtly or by demonstration is: "How do I bring all of these age old truths into my day-today life?" So the *Permission to Practice Activity Journal,* was born.

Permission to Practice is where we really learn to give ourselves Permission to bask in the discovery process and it is where the real results take form. It is the dance of discovering your power, *in action*. The practice journal is all about doing for yourself and learning from first-hand experience rather than just reading about mine or someone else's experience.

Along the way, from simply using the journal for myself and clients to now having it available in several forms, I've discovered I'm actually less of a misfit than I'd initially thought! It seems there are many people genuinely wanting to *practice* and discover a deeper connection to their essence; they only need to discover how.

It is this practice, every day, and especially in the moments when I am experiencing who I *don't* want to be that provides me with the freedom, joy and happiness we are all worthy of. It is being in the moment, naked and raw, and loving my own courage to stand there in the chill of the night that provides me the proof I am far from weak. It is in your realization you are just like the rest of us, amazing and mere mortals, desiring the unconditional love that is yours to give and receive, but sometimes reaching out to places that no longer serve you. It is this willingness to hold your vulnerability with a gentle embrace that provides you the safe platform in which to reach higher to achieve your soul's great desires.

The Practice Journal provides more examples, ideas, information and activities you can practice in your day-to-day life. I recommend you record your experiences in the spaces provided in the journal so you might become more conscious of your own thoughts, feelings, choices and behavior—your *falling in love* with who you are by nature.

Become more aware of what is working for you in your life and what isn't. What do you really want to experience in this lifetime? What would authentic power look and feel like to you…and how might you block yourself from ever experiencing it? When do you feel safe, happy, peaceful and in a place of love? When do you feel defensive, angry, hurt and in a place of fear?

PART TWO the process

Awareness makes room for change and growth.

The Dance of Heightened Awareness Simplified in Five Steps:

1. Acknowledge your thoughts and behaviors

2. Assess each without judgment

3. Magnify anything that serves

4. Release anything that blocks

5. Enjoy the process

6. Repeat, repeat, repeat

Practice Removing Limitations

Our egos are always finding ways to sabotage our success. When I know I am drawn to something yet I refuse to move forward with it (for example the years I fought-off doing yoga even though it popped up time and time again as something that would support my much needed body and spirit connection), I try to simply start with awareness of my blockage, acknowledge my ego's fear, and proceed by removing the perceived obstacles. Many of the exercises in this book will support your opening up to greater awareness of how you might be subconsciously sabotaging your own deepest desires.

As the good Doctor Phil McGraw says,

"You cannot change what you do not acknowledge."

I'd like to add:

You cannot acknowledge what you are completely unaware of.

And you will not choose to see what is deeply hidden in the darkness of fear.

Personal Development is a social activity

There is a very good reason why we can read all of the self-help books in the world and never make one single solid change in our lives. Reading stimulates our *intellectual self*. One of the problems I have with using reading as our main form of self-development is because it is rare that our reasons for being stuck have anything at all to do with the intellectual self but more likely to our emotional self. It is extremely easy to use the intellectual self to sabotage or block us from having to feel; hence we create the busy brain that most humans on earth are currently engaged in.

Maybe if I just read another book, or work harder, or keep busy enough, or understand more, or become more successful I will avoid having to go through the process required **to experience the life I came here to live**. Maybe then I will avoid feeling the pain and the fear of everything that has been locked away since I first discovered my childhood ability to put things into locked compartments.

The irony of our (subconscious) thinking in this way is that we merely *prolong* the fear and the pain. I hope you will challenge, test and play with the ideas I am presenting to you. In this way, you can decide your own truth, which is the whole point of the *Permission* series.

Children learn more in the first two years of their lives than any two years to follow. They are completely self-indulgent. Open. Absorbing. Yearning for touch and love. Interactivity is essential to this time of accelerated growth. Take this connection away from the same children and growth will become more sluggish.

All too often us 'grown-ups' forget the importance of playing together. Does it make us somehow; better people if we drown ourselves in work, family responsibility and whatever else we find busying our lives? Play more and grow faster!

Interaction is how we learn. Reading books, going to seminars and even writing books about personal development does not provide the interactivity necessary to *know* something to be true for you. You can *think* it to be true. You can *believe* it is true. However to *know* something you experience it for yourself.

Experience is what we're doing here in this place we call "our lives". This is the very gift of life itself. We get to play together; we can learn, grow, share and discover who we are in the middle of all this interactivity. We can also choose to battle it out in a war zone. It's just a lot less fun.

I encourage you to use the activities in *Permission to Practice* as a basis for workshops, family discussions, work places, social groups and anywhere you can find the opportunity to practice guilt-free growing up for grown-ups! Especially I hope you will allow yourself to play with some like-spirited people. They make the dance a lot more entertaining, and enjoyment is the greatest motivator there is.

People make us feel! They may not always inspire the feelings we "like," but they help us unveil our true-self in ways we very often cannot discover all alone. What would I do without my playful dance partners? Discovering you really, really, really are not alone can be immensely helpful and healing in itself. When you feel *up* and someone else is *down,* your words of encouragement remind you of how strong you are, and you remind another of how worthy they are to be loved when they fall down. When it is your turn to fall down and be picked up by another, you are reminded of your own worth and your own humanness. Do this thing together wherever possible.

Check out www.gaylamaxwell.com for more opportunities to connect with others.

Ex 5c   **Group Game – Spot the Dead Ender**

Dancing in the Dark

In any relationship, including the relationship we are having with ourselves, we have a few directions in which we can travel, and most of us tend to use up the whole dance floor! On the one hand we can be light on our feet, connected, flowing, kind, and filled with joy; then suddenly without warning Dr. Jekyll comes out to boogie in the blackness! Someone sits in front of you blocking your view in the theater, or you go home for Christmas and suddenly you morph into the angry thirteen-year-old you once were though you were absolutely sure you healed that disturbed adolescent years ago! Something happens that presses **THAT** button and often when it is least expected we become completely irrational, disconnected, cruel, angry and/or in pain.

The fact is, sometimes we're groovin' in love, other times we're shakin' our tail feathers in fear. It depends on how we dance within the relationship to a particular person and or situation.

Somewhere down the long and winding road I figured out that to really know the truth about the loving being that I am by nature, I must not only focus on the *pure* aspect of myself, but also become more aware of, and to acknowledge and accept the part of myself that struggles in a world where fear seems more real than love. Yes, I know it too well. That would be the part of myself that yells in frustration at the elderly driver who obviously feels the world is rushing past him too quickly if he were to drive at the allocated speed limit. That would be the same part of me that sabotages my success and keeps me holding on to behaviors that no longer serve my best intentions. I call this part of myself the darkness, the shadow, the ego, or simply put—it is my fear.

One very important aspect of discovering our true potential is found inside the act of giving ourselves *Permission to Dance* both in the light shades and the shadows of our humanness—because the fact is, we're going to dance in the dark from time to time regardless. I have yet to meet anyone who has never experienced a part of the self that is their darkness. By rejecting this truth, we live in denial of an aspect of ourselves that needs love and acceptance more than anything. It is my experience as we acknowledge and embrace our dark places, we shine light on our fears, and in this way we support their healing.

PART TWO the process

I must say I was pretty excited about this simple discovery when it was first presented to me. It was several years ago while I was practicing the exercises found in *A Course in Miracles,* a book based on what is best known as *spiritual psychotherapy*. It made complete sense to me that all I have to do is bring my darkness (fear) into the light (love) and, miraculously it can no longer be dark! Light out-powers the dark. Simple. Logical. I loved it!

Let me make it clear that I am not merely referring to the age old process of looking into our childhood and seeing how our parents, friends and family have supposedly scarred us for life, though I do accept that the story in itself does have some level of importance. I am talking about looking inside ourselves with open eyes and taking responsibility (not to be read as blame), for what we have done to ourselves *because* of the story.

If my love for, and curiosity about, the human condition has taught me anything, it's that everyone who was born has a story. There is a certain challenge for all of us to exist happily and at peace in a world that is so grounded in fear. Most people (including our parents) know a lot more about experiencing fear and pain whilst on earth, and how to protect themselves from it, than they do about their natural state of harmony and balance.

So given that we all share the same challenge, that is to heal from our wounds in order to radiate our natural power, why is it that some people struggle so much, while others seem to sail through? Does more pain as a child mean more pain as an adult?

In his book *Man's Search for Meaning,* Victor Frankl, a Jewish prisoner of war who was held in a concentration camp during World War II, demonstrates that volume of pain has little or nothing at all to do with how we choose to feel. He said that the enemy could take away everything from the prisoners. They could take their food, their families, their clothes, but they could not take away their right to process their situation with dignity.

> **"EVERYTHING CAN BE TAKEN AWAY FROM A MAN BUT ONE THING;**
>
> the last of the human freedoms—
> to choose one's attitude in any
> given set of circumstances,
> to choose one's own way.
>
> *– Victor Frankl*

I believe the actual details of our life story is of less importance than the understanding of what we *do* with the details. How the child in us processes information will most often be how we will process information as adults until we decide to do it differently. The irrational, stomping, angry, shy, disconnected fearful little human that comes out in us from time-to-time (maybe more often than not in some cases!) is only the child within us that needs to be heard. And he/she will act-out in whatever way he/she needs to in order to get our attention.

With the best of loving intentions, there is no parent who can meet every single tiny need in the child they brought to earth. In the perfect plan, they're not even supposed to! Our life experiences have served us perfectly. Our task is to notice. If you had every need met instantly as a child, you would find it hard to exist in the world for a whole lot of other reasons! (Have you ever spent time with a really spoiled child/adult?)

In the end, each one of us is left with the responsibility of discovering who we are. By listening to the part of ourselves that has yet to be heard, we discover a big piece of that missing information. I discovered simply by having a relationship with the child inside who is screaming to be heard, can in itself stop many self-sabotaging thoughts, feeling and actions.

Compassion is King

Well, I might have thought I had discovered the answer to the entire world's problems with my very simplistic understanding of releasing the ego through living in love. Yet when bringing my new and exciting understanding into my friendships, my family and my consulting work, I soon discovered few people were as excited by this as I was!

It was quickly pointed out to me that if we were all going to be doing some dancing in the dark, they wanted some reassurance they weren't going to be defenselessly bumping and grinding with their Boogie Men!

In other words, if we are to eradicate the defensive wall that has been so diligently constructed to guard against (translation—*to hide*) our fears, our pain and the stories of the past that have proven the need for such a wall in the first place, what happens then? Why would we choose to break down a wall that took years to construct? A wall that we believe is our protection.

How will we treat ourselves if we face our own denial, the ways in which we have sabotaged our own joy and yet blamed others for the misfortune, the "bad" experiences? What are the consequences of taking full responsibility for our own lives?

Okay Boogie Man...Let's Boogie!

If we are to bring to the fore the messy bits that are born of our ego/fear, are we not going to experience more pain, shame, guilt, and further self-loathing? It would be understandable then that *denial* is a lot easier than further self-rebuke. If we don't know it's broken we don't have to fix it—(even if it is unconsciously sabotaging our very chance at having true contentment in our lives!)

I realized this wasn't something that bothered me. Once I understood all I needed to do was to remain self-centered (centered in true-self) enough to *observe, acknowledge* and *embrace* my darkness in order to let it go, that's pretty much what I chose to do. Up until that time, I was a master at self-abuse; and still at times I forget to take care of myself as well as I could. Sometimes it seems we live in a world that rewards self-neglect, unless of course our self-focus involves the purchase of cosmetics to keep us looking age twenty-six up until our eightieth birthday!

It seems to make natural sense to me that to feel safe enough to expose, acknowledge, accept and embrace *all* that we are as a soul having a very human experience—even if only to ourselves—we must learn the skill of **observing our lives as a spectator.**

"*I discovered that rather than finding a place in the outside world through dysfunctional behavior,* **what my inner child really sought was to find refuge in my true-self.**"

– Joanna, Client

I often ask people to be as kind to themselves in their process of growing-up as they would to a small child learning to walk. To observe our ego without judgment, it requires we step away from past learning about *good* and *bad* while opening up to a new way of viewing what might appear to be "wrong." I said might *appear* to be wrong.

Most of us tend to enjoy the forward movement; that is the times in our lives when we can see our growth coming into actualization, heightened intuition, gentleness, happiness, peacefulness and joy. Yet we tend to berate ourselves (overtly or subtly) for the times when we fall down, or seemingly stand still, go backward or take a sideways maneuver. These things we judge as bad.

I now accept with open arms that my journey toward knowing greater acceptance of myself and for others includes these backward and sometimes painful steps in order that I might be given the opportunity to see myself in love and in fear, in joy and in pain. When I personally embraced this concept I discovered I am more capable of making a conscious choice as to where I want to be and how I want to learn. I am also more receptive to the teachings that others offer me, rather than feeling defensive, silly or weak because of my need to grow up further in one way or another.

PART TWO the process

It can be easy to become a know-it-all when we know a little; yet how much more humbling and valuable it is to sit back, observe and discover this the more we learn? The more we know the more we know how *little* we know! As I choose to be kind to myself in this process of never ending awakening, I find it easier to acknowledge my fears. If I need to fall down to learn, I will. If I don't, the lessons are exciting, gentle and often quite humorous!

To practice being more kind to yourself as you learn and grow, have a play with the following exercises:

Ex 2a-c   **Observation vs. Judgment**

Ex 6a-c   **Replacing Fear with Love Inner Child Meditation**

Using the Fall to *Spring* back!

Ironically most people actually choose more often to learn from pain than from joy. Think about it. How often do you stop and take stock of what you can learn from the bright red roses and the exciting romance in a relationship. Yet when it comes crashing down into a painful ending, red roses reduced to fallen petals, sharp dried out thorns and brittle stems in a rubbish bin, we are suddenly reminded of the importance of staying true to ourselves and following our own dreams. How often do we learn from our good health, but when diagnosed with cancer, the reasons we're on this earth become painfully clear? This need not be the way in which we learn. We can equally choose to learn from joy, and this is the reason for becoming more conscious of where we are now, what we are creating in our lives, and how we want to grow.

Nevertheless we can only work with where we are right now, and in that place our choice to fall down or take a few steps back as we grow can serve as another wonderful opportunity. It is tremendously easy to feel all the sensations of love for someone when they seem to be *getting things just right* for you. However, it is much more challenging to dig in and find when they are pressing all of your fragile and wounded buttons. Yet this is when love has the most power to support the healing of old wounds.

I have learned to give myself permission to be the best and the worst of myself. Some days I find it blissfully easy to be kind, feel at peace, to meditate, take great care of myself, and to do the same for others. The good days are a walk in the park. I find myself naturally quite loveable (just between you and me!) There are other days that are simply not that straightforward. It is on those days I learn to love myself and others the best—on the days where my *love handles* are pinching my back and I didn't do my exercises because I found some creative and seemingly valid excuse (such as I had to shampoo the dog and then of course the poor little fella could hardly go for a walk in the cold). That would probably be the same day as I'd cry because someone or another could not understand me in ways I have yet to understand myself, and the toast crumbs left on the kitchen sink (again) courtesy of my daughter were the absolute last straw.

On these days, I have to focus on giving myself permission to be human and love and laugh at myself just as I am. I discovered that as I do so, the anger and the self-sabotage seem to melt away far more quickly than if I had emotionally hammered myself for emotionally thumping myself! On these days I am given the greatest opportunity. *Because* I am being kind to myself and acknowledging how I feel, I can see myself as a loving, playful person who I actually find enjoyable to be with!

Of course when I do fall into my own darkness, fear, or anger, I am also conscious this is not an excuse to abuse the world and leave it worse off because I was there! It is important that we choose to use the moment to change our focus from negative, destructive thought and action to a state that serves our desired outcome. I find that by using laughter or more quietly, the breathing techniques practiced in some forms of yoga, meditation, tai chi, I am able to bring myself back to my natural state of peace more quickly. On the other hand I may use my awareness of buttons being pushed to alert me that a part of me needs nurturing, choosing to go into my feelings more deeply for the purpose of healing.

To know who I am and discover my potential is to know myself warts and all and be able to stand firmly in the Light, knowing that *I am good enough* right in this moment. Trusting that if I could have done better, I would have…and I will. Bit by bit, better and better.

Each time I choose love over fear, and especially in the moments where fear is overwhelming me, I prove to myself that I am loveable, just as I am. As I do so, I feel the same compassion for others… quite naturally.

Breathing techniques can be found on my website, and in your **Permission to Practice Activity Journal**.

Gently nurture the parts of yourself
That hide afraid in the darkness

Give yourself **permission** to enjoy
The **entire** dance.

Unveil the blessing that you are:
So many pieces concealed behind the nooks and crannies
that have gone ignored and unappreciated.

PART TWO the process

Love thyself as you love thy neighbor

I had spent many years watching and supporting the self-development of others. I would teach the importance of self-love and self-acceptance, passionately sharing my belief that we are motivated by only two emotions, these being love and fear. I was then, and continue now to be, inspired by each individual's ability to make a significant difference, if only they knew *what* and *how*. Well, they say that the teacher teaches what they most need to learn. How true those words ring in my ears.

Ever since I can remember, long before my adult years, I have been helping others give themselves permission to move forward, to let go, to dream, to have and be it all; permission to be the dark and the light parts of themselves, so they might experience the love they often unknowingly give to others, while forgetting themselves.

Throughout those years, I believed that playing a part in the awakening of others was all I truly desired. I was an excellent coach and spectator—I had front row seats at the game of everyone else's life. The people on my *team* woke up, they connected, they achieved and they found joy. Inevitably the day came when they would offer back to me their natural gifts. Surprise! And I would feel excited, rejoicing in their achievement; happy and grateful for their offering to this world. And yet at the same time, I would feel ashamed about my own secret. I could see the beauty, the joy and the great gift each and every one of them brought with them, and yet more often than not I struggled to see my own.

I continued to learn more about how human beings spend a lifetime seeking the love they believe is lost somewhere. I studied, observed and absorbed. I was a *born inspiration*, so I was told. That phrase sounded nice to the ear, though it was accompanied by little feeling at all. I couldn't feel it because I couldn't seem to consistently do the same for *myself*.

I remember days when I felt so frustrated I would scream out to whatever or whoever might be out there listening, "Why can't you just send me someone like me?" I wanted someone who could give me what I became aware I had the ability to give to others. I saw the results. These people felt truly loved and accepted. I wanted someone to do that for me! As I write these words today I still laugh at the irony. I wanted a…*me*. I wanted *me*. How would I know for sure I had the ability to inspire others if I had never actually given this gift of inspiration to myself? I had no idea what it felt like to be loved by *me*.

```
I knew the love I sought
was the love I already
had inside of myself.

It was natural that I wanted me.
```
And of course, **you want you.**

Think about the things you do out of love for others. Wouldn't those very same actions make *you* feel loved? We want to receive what it is that we give. The secret to *loving more and needing less* lies in giving the love we give to others back in our own direction. The amazing thing is, as the universal puzzle is affected by your acts of love for yourself, you will soon discover others acting more loving toward you as well. It works! Don't ask me why. I'm not a metaphysics expert but you can prove it to yourself.

I also discovered it was no fluke that I was unable to find any other coach or counselor who worked quite like I did. I really had come to think I was the best there was! While I believe I am not too bad at what I do, let's face it, there is always someone who has more knowledge or someone who can do it better! But I was just perfect for *me*. I wanted a piece of what I so willingly gave to others and so unknowingly denied myself. In the end, we all crave our own love, and nothing can feel as good as the love we give to ourselves. If we are unable to love ourselves, we are unable to fully receive and/or feel the love of others. Nothing will be enough.

Ex 8f-g   **Observing & Honoring Your Uniqueness**
Ex 13a-d   **Who do you think You Are?**
Ex 14a-c   **Self-Acceptance and Self love**

PART TWO the process

The Teacher and Student …
One and the Same

I had some tools in my back pocket so I shared them and you proved they could build dreams.

In my absolute truth, I know it was often through my *clients'* courage I was moved to take a loving spoonful of my own medicine. Just between you and me…I believe most people in emotional care-providing professions started out there to heal themselves if they're really honest; but I'm careful who I say that in front of…or at least I used to be!

It occurred to me that by passing on the tools and simply providing a platform for my clients to know unlimited success, I was able to witness *their* successes; over and and over and over again. I saw that what was possible was in fact quite infinite! The teacher and the student are one and the same. I always remember that. It will serve you well to do the same. Don't just pay it lip service like so many of the spiritual teachers I've witnessed. Suck it up into your humble little veins! If ever I even get a whiff of thinking I am anybody's guru, something sure enough comes along to remind me: **Nobody is of greater or lesser value in their ability to contribute to the same instant.**

Somewhere into my adult life I came to realize and then finally *accep*t I have always seen the world a little differently to what might be considered the 'norm'. I used to strongly resent that about myself. My grandmother used to buy me owls; stuffed owls, ornaments and broaches, all reminding me of my so called wisdom. I just felt different. To say I didn't always fit in at the dinner party or group social events would be an understatement. Yet when I allow myself to go with the flow of who I am by nature, I am inspired, I am happy, and I am able to share that with others. Sometimes the things we like least about ourselves are the very things that are our greatest gifts.

I believe many of us abandon ourselves, leaving undiscovered the full potential within ourselves; hoping that by being nice, good, kind, and giving to others, we might get the same in return. If we're completely honest, we quietly hope to get back the love and kindness we give to others. This might actually work for a while, but eventually the neediness will be exposed.

> Join to others without need,
> but acknowledge that together two are greater than one.
> Offer the same goodness, kindness, and understanding to yourself
> as you give to your Beloved,
> and there will not exist a need for anything…
> There is only unconditional love.

> "You can search the entire universe for somebody more worthy of *your love* than you, and you will never find them."
>
> – Buddha

It is inevitable we *will* discover love and great happiness within ourselves if only we get *there* to look for it... *within ourselves*. I decided I was no longer going to try to move around these wounds by "healing others" and watching from the sidelines. I knew I had to go through my own darkness, proving it to be weaker than my determination to live in greater peace and joy. I would consciously and completely commit to giving them all the open space that they needed to heal. (By the way, the wounds might sting for a little while when you first allow them fresh air to heal, but you can rest assured they will most certainly fester and grow under the surface if you don't.)

An inspirational man who I had the pleasure of working with doing children's entertainment some years ago gave me the best analogy I have ever heard in relation to the power of shining light on our fear. He said;

"If you sit in complete darkness and then light only one small match, the darkness loses its power. It exists no longer. And so it is as you shine the light of love on your own darkness. It loses its power to hold you in fear, and you will be illuminated, and you will know the source of true power."

PART TWO the process

A Good Dancer is Not Without Bruises

Like the rest of us, you will most likely fall flat on your no longer nappy padded butt more than once as you trip over some of the more challenging steps of your unique dance. You will get confused, be too tough on yourself and others, feel excited, feel frustrated, and wonder if you're getting anywhere at all. Welcome to the dance floor.

When you were learning how to walk for the first time, you had someone there to keep putting you back on your feet (if you were lucky). This time, it's just you. *You* are the encouragement, the love, the support and the gentle touch you need throughout this process. If you slap yourself every time you fall down, you will only stunt your growth and slow down the very process you are hoping to achieve.

Over a particular period of time I found myself repeatedly saying to my clients and my friends, "you need to be more loving to yourself!" I would see their blank looks of confusion. Many of you reading this book might just need to learn *how* to be your own support system. God knows I have learned the long, drawn out, slowest possible way imaginable—and I must continue to practice awareness every day.

We must relearn how to walk before we dance because much of what we learned, with all the best of intentions by our teachers, was limited by fear. Then we grow up not only fearing the pain of bruises themselves; we fear our own shame that we actually became bruised! Cruel really don't you think?

We have learned to be good, to put one foot in front of the other just like everybody else. Most of us have learned to be aware of everybody else's feelings but our own. We learned not to step on the toes of our dance partners, but rarely were we taught how to explore our own *unique dance;* how to be comfortable in our own skin and how to move to our own rhythm.

Have you ever noticed most people are *not* choosing to take the step to discover what is possible in their very unique life? Most choose to follow. It's easier. It provides less reward and less potential for contribution, but certainly it is familiar. So who *does* choose to fully embrace the unique life they came here to experience? Who finds the courage?

I've found in my practice, the common thread linking people choosing to live more consciously is that they are less comfortable with where they are *now* and they sense "there must be more" or "there must be a better way". The feeling of remaining stuck is a less appealing option than doing what they need to do to have the life they want. In fact I test people's discomfort level when they come to see me so I can gage how successful we're going to be. If they're too comfortable in their pain, preferring to hold onto their 'stories' than do what it takes to create new ones, we have one session.

There is nothing quite like a little bit of discomfort, times of change and/or instability to open our receptiveness to taking greater control of our lives, even if it's just taking control of this one thought in this one moment. People going through marriage separations, depression, job changes, loss of a loved one, financial concerns and any other time of uncertainty tend to be more willing to open to their fundamental need to be connected to their true Self. They are willing to do something different in order to get new results.

> ***Is some part of your outside world finally uncomfortable enough for you to do something different about the relationship you're having with your inside world?***

You are all you can control, and the rest will happen as it does. In taking control there are a few things you're going to need in high doses. I've been practicing this work for a long time, as have many of my clients and I assure you, without these three things, taking control is a tough gig! We explore how we can increase all of these qualities throughout the book but for now, just ask yourself if you already have these attributes in abundance, or if you might want to expand them as you dance!

Your Dance Kit should include:

1. DETERMINATION:

The pain of staying stuck outweighs the fear of moving forward. Please understand I am not meaning that you must stay in pain. I am suggesting when there is a choice between falling into old patterns in your mind or embracing the new more healthy choice for yourself, you choose the latter. I can give you all the formulas; practical tools to use but only you can use them. When we have come to the end of our patience with feeling whatever negative emotions we are feeling: lost, alone, fearful, limited, lonely, etcetera, then we move forward. Without this ingredient of determination, I know as soon as I tell a client I will only be as committed to them as they are, it will probably be our last appointment—until the pain of staying stuck outweighs the fear of moving forward. The amount of pain you need is up to you. Sometimes I've needed a bucket (times a hundred) to move away from that which no longer serves me. I don't recommend it but it's your dance! With the tools I'm about to share, you can choose to use them as soon as you become aware something no longer serves you, or you can wait until you're sick or you become more uncomfortable in some other way. Determination will at some point set in if you are to have all that you deserve and desire.

2. ACCEPTING OF THE GIFT OF OUR HUMANNESS:

From time to time as we grow, we get messy. If things don't get a little out of place on occasion, it is unlikely we're doing the really deep, core, life-altering stuff. That's the real deal.

I was speaking to my sister this morning and we were discussing those people who seem to absolutely cruise through this life. They don't appear to do a lot of growing nor providing contribution to a world in need of greater peace. Yet somehow life seems to work out fine and diddly-dandy for these cohabitants of our dear planet. Effortlessly they plod; taking, using and on surface level appear to have no concern for anyone but themselves. Often very liberal with their own judgment, they generously remind us, (passively or overtly) that the struggles we seem to face in our own very humble, sometimes untidy lives… are clearly our own "fault".

Do you know the fine folk I refer to here?

Without hesitation, in fact by interruption my sweet and way too wise sister hit me with this one… "I really believe those people are just here this time around to ruffle the feathers of those of us choosing to learn a lot. They're here solely to help us get to the next level of our own evolution." She finished by saying, "how very generous these good souls are to offer a whole lifetime to *our* awakening…don't you think?"

Now if that isn't the clear demonstration of *acceptance of the gift of our humanness*, I don't know what is!

If we can see ourselves, and others doing the best we can do on any given day, with each person being an offering to our own learning, life becomes easier. All we can expect of ourselves in the face of any situation is to be the best we can be, right here and now.

Without compassion for ourselves and for others, the dance is made unnecessarily more painful, bumpy and quite frankly, too unpleasant for some of us more rebellious dancers to be bothered at all!

Self-acceptance always spills into greater acceptance of others. Imagine how much easier life would be if we truly believed it was not our responsibility to be the judge and jury in our own lives and the lives of others. This doesn't mean we condone every behavior. We simply choose not to judge the *person* for the behavior. In fact the behavior itself wouldn't be presented to us at all if we didn't ask to observe it.

We will have a close look at how we can take more control of this "law of perfect attraction" in the upcoming Dance of Opportunity and in your *Permission to Practice Activity Journal*.

When we stop to observe with honesty just how much we unnecessarily judge and condemn, it can be quite an eye-opener even for the most seasoned dancer! Letting go of this one thing alone…is one of the most powerful steps toward power and ultimate freedom.

And last but not least…

3. A MIGHTY FINE SENSE OF HUMOR:

We are hilarious. Really we are. We *must* laugh at ourselves or we will fall more often and suffer blacker, bigger and sorer bruises. Lighten up and laugh. Get back up, learn from the experience and laugh some more.

> *"Guts, compassion and a little laughter not only makes all things possible, it makes achieving them an enjoyable process"*

As we learn the secrets of moving to our own rhythm, we inevitably find aspects of ourselves, and the world around us that we would prefer to have kept hidden back stage. Reminding ourselves of how "stupid" we were to create the painful situations in the first place is only a detour on our path to peace. Most of us take the detours from time-to-time. The point is to understand they are only detours, not the road to where you really want to go.

It has taken time, a little discomfort, a lot of laughs mixed with some significant effort, but each step that I have practiced, each move that caused some pain, has taught me the joy of fully embracing this dance of a lifetime. I used to ask for *permission;* seeking from others the approval that only I can provide; permission to be just as I am. Now I understand by the very nature of the human experience, we not only have *permission* to experience the fullness of our being, we have a *responsibility*.

How good it feels to give ourselves all-encompassing permission to be all that we are. In the process, by taking complete responsibility for our own lives, we also allow others to be all they can naturally be. Then and only then, do we have that fullness of our being to offer to others. Then we have the power to change things.

PART TWO the process

May you always remember to

Embrace the courage,

Feel the grace

And bask in the joy

as you dance
to your own rhythm

PART **THREE**

I like to call this one 'OPPORTUNITY!'

the dance of OPPORTUNITY

7 steps

in the Dance of Opportunity

Using Relationships to Unveil True Love

1. Take one step backward
Observe without judgment—observe with compassion and acceptance.

2. Look up, look down, look left and right, now look inside
Check your intentions—override your ego and get to the truth.

3. Stand and hold the position with your head held high
Acknowledge what you have co-created—the good the bad, the beautiful and the ugly.

4. Turn and face your partner
Take responsibility for your contribution.

5. Take two steps forward
Do something toward healing the past you are trying to recreate.

6. Extend both your hands
Accept the fullness of the gifts the person, the situation and the experience had to offer.

7. Shake your Tail Feather!
Feel the gratitude—you get it! And your dance partner helped to make that possible.

PART THREE the dance of opportunity

The steps are gentle and easy— *choosing to use them* is up to you...

As we apply these 7 steps, eventually leading us to feel grateful for some of our more challenging relationships and or experiences, we gently let go of past pain, allowing it to serve as a tool for greater wisdom rather than a crutch that leads us to believe we are somehow wounded and in need of fixing.

One of the greatest revelations I recall coming to, was that as I danced with each relationship I encountered, and maintained focus on using the opportunity to grow, I knew that all things great and small, good and bad, could directly serve my own awakening to a greater place of joy. In this I knew, there is really nothing to forgive myself or anyone else for. We were just dancing, in service to one another's awakening.

In theory it seems like a relatively simple dance don't you think? So if it is that easy, does it not lead to the question,
"Why isn't everyone shakin' their tail feather?"

The Qualities of a Conscious Dancer

Each person, place and thing

Each relationship we have with all things great and small

Are given to us as a dance partner,

and together we embrace

The Dance of Opportunity

Discovering the greatest Self we can possibly be

I am of the full belief that each moment is a gift offered to support our discovery of true love. Not necessarily the kind of so called "true love" found in romantic novels though this can also be true, but rather the authentic, unconditional love that needs no romance, nor is it always wrapped up in pretty bows. It needs nothing but itself.

Some people will choose to dig in and immerse very consistently and consciously and therefore discover more abundance and gratitude than they could ever have imagined. They smell it in the trees, taste it in the rain, feel it in a touch and they can even see it in the eyes of a criminal—because they are looking. They discover the magic of each moment and the opportunity that it is to embrace a greater connection with the love that is within themselves.

Those of us who make that choice understand that to find true love, we will make loving choices at times when fear is gripping at our hearts, but we know the laws of the universe—*as ye sew so shall ye reap.* So with courage we learn to face and overcome our fears and we receive that love.

As discoverers of this unconditional love we are reminded to be gentle with ourselves in moments when we fall down, understanding that our fall is an indication of the need for nurturing, and so we nurture ourselves. Undoing old habits of self-criticism can be challenging, but certainly possible to overcome! *Conscious* dancers trust that every situation we find ourselves in is created from our own desire to learn, and so we embrace both the challenging relationship and gentle one as equal opportunities to enhance our dance of *greater knowing.* And we dance with each partner like it may be the last time our feet touch the ground!

PART THREE the dance of opportunity

Do We Have to be Perfect to Find True Love?

Let me start by saying something that I have found to be my greatest comfort, *we are* perfect. We may have learned a few nasty little habits. And we may suffer a little bit of self loathing from time to time; some anger, frustration, jealousy, depression and a wealth of other emotions that drive our temporary behavior and outcomes. But each of us has essentially been designed perfectly to bring to the dance floor of life, what only we as individuals can bring.

I'm sure you're getting by now that unveiling our true essence and learning self-love is in no way a life of rules and notions of having to be *good* or *spiritual* all the time. In fact it is about being *real* and recognizing this is the most spiritual thing we can do! Our task is not to *become* perfect by doing a lot of "good" things, but rather to discover our natural perfection that hides beneath layers of fearful behavior and beliefs. We do this by *observing* what's already right, not ridiculing what we perceive is wrong!

You are exactly where you are meant to be in this moment, reading this book, on that train, in that lounge room, overweight, underweight, single, married—happily or unhappily. Wherever you are, it is as it needs to be in this moment—and this moment is specifically designed *by* you *for* you. This is the place in which you have chosen to pick up a book called *Permission to Dance*. So it is in this place where our dance *together* occurs. It can be joyous or painful—even how you choose to experience it need not be judged.

Finding *Perfection* through Connection

I think this concept of perfection was one of the most difficult for me to grasp. I thought to myself, "If I created this mess I was living in and I was totally depressed in the middle of it all… how could everything be perfect?" I resented the very thought of having so much power over my own life because clearly I was doing a pretty lousy job of managing it! It took the best part of ten years for me to move from resentment of the concept to living each day in accordance with it. I can't imagine living any other way now. I know which way of living feels better to me…and I know which way of living gives me the power to create as I choose. It certainly isn't by staying disempowered by fear and resentment.

Gradually we become better at taking responsibility for our choices. I now know it could have taken a lot **less** time! I realized these choices were occurring every minute of my life. I could choose how I viewed someone, how I responded to them, how I felt about a red light, or a traffic fine. What happens when we really decide to live in connection with perfection (if you will pardon the rhyme) is that we are able to ease-up on the overactive brain that tries to control our environment. Now I tell my brain what's going to occur rather than the other way around!

The Law of Perfect Attraction

One of the most exciting discoveries I have made on my own search is the *law of perfect attraction*. I am very conscious in my writing not to dictate the *rules according to Gayla* because I have read one too many such books myself, however some things in life just simply *are*. Don't shoot the messenger as they say. There are universal rules that apply every time, and one of these is *the law of perfect attraction*. We will attract exactly what we need in order to grow, learn, be rewarded…to discover and develop our own unique dance.

The Universal Matchmaker

I imagine universal energy like the perfect dance school which has great expertise in knowing exactly what step each individual at the school requires most practice in. It also knows the precise dance partner—or at least the dance partner(s) who right now will best serve them to learn this step. Even more perfectly (this is that thing called *synchronicity* that just gets me every time), this perfect dance school knows that the particular step being learned together will perfectly benefit both or all partners who will practice together for each step a dance partner is selected. Sometimes we dance with one partner to learn many lessons and sometimes one lesson is so challenging for that individual or both partners that several partners are called in to assist.

PART THREE the dance of opportunity

So what does all this dancing mean in our day-to-day life?

Simply put, it means when you are challenged by a particular situation with friends, family, work colleagues or strangers, it is not the people surrounding you who are causing the "problem." Though your ego would happily point the finger in their direction, it is *you* who is struggling to accept the lesson that is being presented.

I have watched many times this, universal matchmaker marry-up individuals who are quite unknowingly asking for ways in which to learn a particular lesson. The lessons themselves can come wrapped up in many differing stories but in the end, each lesson seems to boil down to one request and that is. *Teach me more about the unconditional love within me so I can live in peace and joy.* Since most of us don't actually believe this to be the truth, it is more often that we will ask for lessons such as, *help me feel less jealous* (so I might know the pure love within me), or *help me feel confident, or compassionate, or peaceful* (so I might know the pure love within me).

Until we learn where the real power center is within ourselves, that place where we actually do have some control over our life outcomes, we find more commonly the requests sent out are for things such as the great job, the hot boyfriend, the bigger boobs and wrinkle free face, the nice car, the record deal, the fame, and whatever else we think might bring us that deep happiness we know somehow rightfully belongs to us, yet we struggle to hold onto for any length of time. And we might get any or all of them! AND they will make great dance partners! They will provide every opportunity we need to grow.

When the ego gets involved (translation: fear), rather than facing the challenge a dance partner provides and experiencing the growing-up process; we ask for the lesson to be removed. *Get that woman/man off my man's stage! She's going to take him away from me and that will mean I'm not as good as she/he is!*

Nobody is judging the choice to focus on avoidance, but it *is* moving away from an issue rather than feeling the fear and using it to grow. Every time we point a finger at another, or believe we have a valid "reason" for inner unrest of any kind, we are in this place of avoidance. If you look around your life, and listen more intently to others, you are likely to observe that most people are validating their inner chaos every day. So judging our avoidance, (otherwise known as our "inner victim") is hardly useful. Becoming aware of how your ego is pushing away an opportunity our button pressers provide rather than using it to grow is a far more useful choice. We will do some practice around how we observe ourselves (and others) without judgment. The longer you dance, the more you will use that tool!

Somewhere there is your perfect dance partner for every lesson. Let's take an example of *impatience*. If you find it hard to be patient, your perfect dance partner might mirror impatience so you experience what it is like to be on the other end of their intolerance. On the other hand, they may behave in such a way that pushes all your buttons and so they test your patience.

Not all and everything is there to teach us through challenge. I've noticed when someone has grown through previous dance partners, becoming more of the patient person their soul yearned to be, they often attract someone or something which provides the perfect example of how far they've come. This dance partner, (be it a situation or a person) no longer needs to press buttons, instead providing a mirror, which demonstrates the growth that has occurred in that individual so far.

These requests for our dance partners most often are not conscious requests we send off to the universe. They come from our deepest soulful yearning to know our own full potential, experiencing ourselves through the reflection of our life, and the people within it. Usually even more powerful than our conscious thoughts, these requests are made from the desires of the soul. And the soul will always seek to support the discovery of every dark space within us in order that it might shine love on the places in need of nurture.

As We Dance Connected Through Synchronicity...
WE GROW TOGETHER

While this idea of perfect dance partners might seem quite impossible in our usual physical way of viewing the world, the law of the universe is amazingly vast and it knows not time, distance nor separation. We are enough and we are perfect dance partners, even when we are unable to see the effect our dance (the chaos and the magic) has on anyone else.

We are working together through our intention to heal even when we cannot physically see those we are connected to. Our task is to learn to trust beyond what we see.

The more you tap into the part of yourself that co-creates through intention, the more able you are to create consciously what you desire and what only you can offer this planet. What do *you* want to create?

PART THREE the dance of opportunity

If you would like to become a better observer in your own life so you are more clear on who you are and what you truly desire, these exercises are good ones to play with:

Ex 9a-n   **Creating the changes you REALLY Desire**

Who Are You Dancing With and Why?

Have a look around you right now. Don't take my word for it; test the theory. Look at the relationships you find difficult, challenging, and/or dysfunctional. Some of these relationships will be "easy to get out of," for example casual friendships, while other relationships will seem almost impossible to remove yourself from, such as your parents or other family members. While none of these relationships are more or less important to your own discovery of your true self, some will certainly be more challenging because we believe we are bound to them. If none of the situations you find yourself in with any of these people is actually *bad*, though, it certainly may not feel very *good* at times, and they could be called in to see who you do not want to be! They are all just opportunities to discover.

The relationships or dance partners we feel are impossible to move away from are the ones in which we have called in to help us stay committed to getting a particular life challenging lesson. It is not actually a fact that the dance must go on forever; however, your belief in that *fact* is the universe's way to help you stick with it until the gift of the lesson becomes your knowing. Note that I say *knowing*, rather than just *thinking*. We can think we have finished learning a particular lesson. We can talk about it, share it with our friends, sound very strong and appear very wise, but the universe acknowledges only our hearts, not our heads. When our heart knows greater love from any particular challenging dance partner, then and only then will the dance truly end. If you abandon that dance partner before the lesson is complete, get ready to welcome the next person who is going to step all over your feet once again. The situation or person might appear to be very different at first, yet before long you will recognize you are waltzing to the same tune only with a different partner. (Don't shoot the messenger!)

I live this reality myself and I know intimately the challenge it can present. What I have also discovered is that to accept your lessons with grace works a lot better than fighting the universe. I've tried. I've put a few dance partners in the rubbish bin because of *their* nasty behaviors. I just moved on to find another person who seemed to have the same nasty behavior. Could it be something I'm attracting, creating and/or developing in my relationships in order to heal something in myself?

Something I certainly discovered through my own trial and error, and that of my many clients is that as we choose to focus on what *we're* doing, what *we* might be fearful of and how *we* might be contributing to the issues at hand, some interesting revelations occur.

We may discover:

- the so called "nasty behavior" sometimes didn't even exist (except in my own head)

- the other person becomes safe enough to explore their own behavior as I take the pressure off them and focus on how I could support rather than blame them

- the behavior no longer bothers me

- the behavior will vanish from the relationship

- the process is an opportunity to unite more intimately the process is an opportunity to move together and yet honor individual lessons

- a new awareness about our own fear and our ego acts in a particular situation

- why we might attract a situation and how it might actually be there to support further awakening rather than being a "bad" thing

And last but certainly not least... **Fighting our opportunities to learn only serves to prolong the agony!**

PART THREE the dance of opportunity

Intimate and Primary Relationships – "The Sticky Ones"

Many of you will recognize this rule of attracting the perfect lesson teachers in your more intimate relationships. I have shared countless consultations with men and women who have revealed to me they thought they had gotten rid of *that spiteful so and so*, only to discover the next guy/girl was bringing up the same issues with a slightly different slant. (I often laugh at how I attract the clients who will also serve my own awakening!)

This applies also to your children, parents, grandparents and your romantic relationships. All are known as *primary relationships* and when they're driving us to despair…we can also think of them as our "sticky relationships" The ones we can't just say good-bye to because they're annoying us today! How many women have told me they feel like they feel like they married their father? It's not fluke ladies!

```
Our primary relationships have the most power to free us.
They also have the potential to inflict the most wounds.
Our task is to use these relationships to heal rather than
remain stuck in pain.
```

Ex 2b-c   **Opportunity to Observe in Primary Relationships**
Ex 4a-b   **Take Responsibility, Release Blame**

Dancing in Pain or Pleasure—It's Our Choice to Learn Either Way!

I have certainly learned that until we shift the belief we are unworthy, we are often likely to attract others who will help us learn through negative means, or at least these will be the opportunities we most recognize. But the universe wants only our highest good, and therefore we are also given as much opportunity to learn through love as through fear or pain. We have equal experience opportunities to see ourselves lovingly through the eyes of someone who loves us. These opportunities can be right in front of us, but we are unable to see them because they don't make sense to us. Have you ever known a woman who is only attracted to the bad boy? Oops, sorry... that's you? How about the man whose spirit wants to experience the gift of unconditional love while his ego continues to lead him straight into the clutches of women who are airbrush perfect, generously endowed, and completely disconnected from themselves. You know the folks I refer to?

I believe one of our greatest tasks is to *choose* to be awake or conscious to the lessons on offer to us. Often we are so wrapped up in the details and the fear we are experiencing we miss the gentle opportunity all together. This gentleness might come in the form of a friend or a stranger who says just the right thing at the right time. It might be in the form of winning a trip so that you are removed from a negative situation and given time to reconnect to your own spirit. When our eyes are open to the generous opportunities, we begin to see and feel the joy of learning in love. Gratitude attracts more reasons to feel grateful!

When we acknowledge our worth, even just a small amount, the universe recognizes this as true love, and continues to mirror our truth by sending more of the same. One of my dear and playful dance partners has always said, "Be it good or bad, we always get back what we give—ten fold!" I'm not so sure of the exact ratio, but I certainly have experienced many times over both the generosity and the intensity of the laws of the universe! We can rest assured if we have something to learn, we will be given more than our fair share of opportunities. Can you recall experiencing that?

As we look for themes or pattern in our own lives we discover some of the lessons our soul is calling out for you to learn.

PART THREE the dance of opportunity

To feel grateful for the relationships currently serving your life today, practice the **walking meditation**. Allow your focus to be solely on how each one of these relationships is of service to your understanding and acceptance of true love into your life today. You may find it more difficult to feel grateful for some relationships than you do for others. Attempt focus on at least one challenging relationship as you allow the gift of appreciation to wash over you.

Ex 14d   **Walking Meditation—Gratitude in Action**

LEARNING FROM PAST DANCES— CHOOSING NOT TO REPEAT PAST PAIN

Whatever we focus on grows.
If we want to repeat the past,
Or we want to receive the gift of this moment
Just focus on it!

Can you think of any time in the past in which a seemingly bad situation or relationship led you to something very positive? A time when you realized you learned from this person or situation and because of that, it/they were of great service to your life?

If your answer is, "absolutely not," then we have a lot of work to do together! And that's okay. If you are reading this book right now, then now is the right time for you to be reading it and practicing the exercises in your *Permission to Practice Journal*. Your awakening will be all the more exciting for you as you open your eyes and see true love in this way for the first time!

For those who are already aware of turning so called negatives into positive life enhancing lessons, then let's have a look at why and how we were able to achieve it quickly. I must also say here that this book is not just a series of positive thinking exercises; quite to the contrary. Rather it is important we identify *how* a situation and/or relationship becomes a life enhancing lesson as opposed to something we simply put into the past, ignoring our true and often hurt feelings while pretending them away with "positive thinking." This way of doing things only insures more toe-stepping and painful dance partners, and who needs the bruises?

While there is some truth to the saying that things just work themselves out naturally with time, you actually have to *do* something different in order to be able to see the positive in a seemingly negative situation. Time can only make a situation appear to be further in the past. To actually *learn* from a relationship and or situation, you are consciously or unconsciously applying some basic skills that when used consistently, can awaken you to the gift that your entire life naturally is; a life that is filled with magical synchronicities and unlimitedly diverse dance partners. As we dance with each partner, allowing ourselves to embrace the opportunity to change our focus from fear to love, from what's wrong to what is a gift, we awaken to the benefits and the power that creates our unlimited, abundant lives.

To get the most from any challenging situation or relationship, we must acknowledge it for the gift it is and allow ourselves to accept this gift to its fullest. As difficult as that might seem at times, it is its own ultimate reward.

If you want to put some of this to the test, a relevant exercise you might like to try in the *Permission to Practice* Activity Journal would be:

Ex 9a-u   **Creating the Changes you REALLY desire**

Ex 14a   **Walking Meditation—Gratitude in Action**

The Shortcut to Finding Greater Happiness and Learning from the Past

EACH MOMENT IN TIME IS A PRECIOUS GIFT THAT I GRANT OR DENY MYSELF.

If you are anything like myself and thousands of other searchers on the planet, we have all looked high and low for a shortcut to finding deep happiness. On my search, I discovered it really is quite simple to know happiness and I have suspected it is in this simplicity that most people get confused. We mere mortals tend to complicate what is so obvious in the law of the universe.

PART THREE the dance of opportunity

I discovered happiness comes from the ability to refocus—to shift my thoughts from fear to love.

Happiness comes from being gentle on myself and on others as we fall down in fear; and it is the joy I feel as we find the faith and courage to stand back up again. It is the knowledge that all things serve a purpose; and all I need do is trust in that law. I needn't even understand the purpose itself; only allow it to unfold.

> *Happiness is not the result of good things happening; it is the result of finding good things in whatever happens and being grateful for the opportunity.*

Since learning this particular truth I find it almost enjoyable to welcome those people who might push my buttons and step on my toes—well, a lot of the time anyway. As I dance with them consciously, allowing myself and them to hit the floor, and get back up without having to beat anyone up with a baseball bat, I find I am genuinely grateful to them by the time the music ends. I admit with some people and situations it might take a whole lot of rehearsal time, but I now believe absolutely there is no dancing around the lessons. If I am to know greater peace and happiness in my life, I am absolutely convinced the short cut is to go straight to the source of love within me.

Through years of conscious searching both within myself and with my clients, I have proven enough times even for me (the ultimate rebel), that unless I find the place within myself that is kind to me, I will find myself in the same place once again. Same dance—different day.

I have come to a place where I am keen to accept the shortcut.

Ex 14a-c   **Self-Acceptance**

How Relationships Serve our Unveiling

> Take a few steps forward,
> take a few steps back.
> Grab a partner to remind you
> when your shoes have gone off track

Given that I do love to dance, the analogy of dancing in relationships made a lot of sense to me. Much like any dance I've ever learned, our relationships provide so many wonderful opportunities to discover and express parts of ourselves. There are the steps themselves, the swaying, and the physical direction in which we move. Then there is the next level of dancing, and this is how we interpret each stride. How *we feel* the movement and whether or not we allow ourselves to discover more about the dancer we are, or choose rather to accuse the choreographer of poor choice when the progression is uncomfortable.

When a performer really uses each subtle motion to uncover and express a piece of their being, it touches the spectator and elevates the dancer.

For most of us mere mortals who don't quite make it to the big stage, we can tend to find ourselves doing a whole lot of shaking, some stepping on toes, a little spinning round and round. Then when it's all over, we're left wondering if we actually got anywhere at all, still on the same smoky dance floor—sometimes feeling as though if we did move, it was backwards!

But we *do* move. With each dip, each sway and each touch of another's hand, we feel something. And it is in this feeling itself we are given great opportunity. When we take up the opportunity to look at our own performance rather, than focus on what we perceive to be the poor delivery of our many dance partners, then we move forward and we unveil a little more authentic power.

I've created seven basic *steps* in the *Dance of Opportunity*. These steps demonstrate the *process* of becoming more conscious so we can create that which we choose, rather than unconsciously create the rubbish we *do not* want in our relationship to ourselves, others and our world. It offers an opportunity to practice connecting to the part of ourselves who is the observer of our actions.

PART THREE the dance of opportunity

Each relationship we have with anyone or anything (including ourselves) is the partner who provides opportunity to move to a higher knowing of who we are at our core. How we choose to dance with each partner directly affects how much or how little we refine our dance techniques, how much we learn, how we grow, and how much true love we will discover in the process.

The dance itself may not always be beautiful to the eye, however perfect in its essence. Each dance partner—that is every situation, every person, every plant or animal or anything else you are in relationship to or with—provides a perfect opportunity to practice seeing a part of who you are. It is in this act of making moment to moment choices to see ourselves as a loving being where we come to know the meaning of true and unconditional love. Suddenly the idea of being worthy or not worthy of love seems ridiculous.

> *Within me lies quietly, without demand*
> *the love that I used to seek through the eye of others.*

This sentence seems less and less *poetic* and more and more *true* as we dance in consciousness.

The dance aims to remind us we are in fact always in relationship, be it the relationship I was having with my computer or the relationship I was having with my teenage daughter who was, at the time of my writing this book on school holidays and popping-in every five minutes to ask for everything from a driving lesson to money for new clothes.

The first relationship I mention, that of the one I am having with my computer, is a fairly benign one. I am grateful for what it offers me in helping me produce this book, and as long as I press the right keys, it seems to be pretty content to serve. The second relationship I mention, the one I was in with my beautiful teenager served me particularly well in that moment in providing a wonderful opportunity for me to observe my own chaos and how I was doing in relation to a couple of other things I'd been focusing on such as; living in the moment, being able to speak my truth gently, remembering what was most important to me and a seemingly simple one but one that surprisingly requires a lot of practice to do properly, breathing! I'm pleased to report; I did all right!

> ** Amendment: Since writing the last paragraph my gorgeous daughter woke up on her birthday and turned that teenage corner everyone promised me she would. Now she actually likes me most of the time! Ah, life. It never stops reminding me that just when I think I know something to be true, my mind must open even further. Nothing stays the same. How wonderful.*

While practicing my own *Dance of Opportunity* I have discovered many new moves and have come to recognize the false poses that no longer serve me. The cover-ups, the denials, the busying myself when the going gets tough and all I really need to do is a simple meditation to bring me back into my consciousness. We all have ways of justifying our ego's need to sabotage.

Sometimes we will need to take a few steps *back,* providing the opportunity to observe without judgment where we are in any given moment, learning the skill of being our own spectator of the dramas and comedies that we create, rather than identifying ourselves as *being* what we create.

Other times we might need to put the *back and side step* into action…this is what I call it when we feel like we're not getting anywhere; not moving forward, not actually going backward, just simply taking some time to allow the new lessons and skills we're learning to sink in and become more natural for us while still practicing the skill of observation. The greatest misconception about becoming self-empowered or more "enlightened" as it is also referred to, is that we must always be moving forward, actively doing something that *appears* to be coming from a place of love. Yet I have discovered as we awaken, we will take just as many steps to the left, to the right and then backwards. If we are gradually mastering the art of spectator, very often we are having to learn to be more still and less active. It might feel like we are in Nowhereville when in truth it is a place where we can enjoy some well-deserved and much needed time out! Oh yes, I know it well.

In relationships, we experience ourselves in all sorts of messy and beautiful ways. *The Dance of Opportunity* is intended to be a way of lightening-up the process of awakening to the part we play. Taking full responsibility for how we contribute to the outcomes within any relationship (without having to add the "but you…" justification clause) can be tricky for most of us. I refer not only to romantic relationships, but those we have with all people, places, situations, and experiences. Relationships are our mirror. They help us see where we are. They push our buttons, and they are the great gift we are given to support our unveiling.

The Myth of the Soul Mate

Soul Mates don't necessarily dance like Fred Astaire.

They will, however, find every aching muscle and weak spot in our bodies,

helping us work through the pain, heal the wounds and make us stronger dancers!

It almost seems cruel to burst the Soul Mate bubble. We have been provided so much amazing and romantic information through fairy tales, magazines, romance novels and almost every romantic comedy ever made in Hollywood, confirming the grass really is greener on the other side. I loved that fairy tale! There must be a Mr. or Mrs. Just Right, right?

PART THREE the dance of opportunity

We have been told over and over that all of us have a soul mate, and the really lucky people actually find that one and only special person! We're told when we do find them, he or she will be the perfect fit. We will be in blissful love forever. And we will live happily ever after. These people want all of the same things we want and they adore absolutely everything about us, as we adore the perfect ground they walk on.

And that's where the Walt Disney movie ends.

I am not suggesting people do not find wonderful partners in life who share great joy.

I am suggesting when the real *love story* begins; it is also most likely to bring with it some trials and awakenings, struggles and fear. It can feel like both our feet are completely off the ground and yet it can also be anything from bittersweet to downright nasty. It can be filled with great joy, wonderful sharing and violent pain. But one thing remains consistent; it always serves our highest purpose if only we choose to see.

Our most intimate relationships are the ones that provide some of the best opportunities; however, this requires that we take responsibility and at times, let's be honest, that is not easy! To love is a choice. It is an action, a state of being, not something that just happens to us. The only part that seemingly happens naturally is the attraction. The rest is a choice to use the attraction to practice greater love or conversely to live stuck in fear.

At first love might seem easy. I mean before you start believing it is *the other person* who has in some way changed for the worse. You see the person for who he or she really is. You see only the loving qualities, the truth, the special smile, the gentleness, the efforts to overcome fear, and you see the goodness within the person. You believe your partner is all of these things because that's what is being shown to you. Your partner feels safe to present a loving self because you are mirroring his or her best. You are not criticizing (yet), judging based on fearful behavior (yet), withdrawing your love (yet). At the same time, you too are presenting your loving self. You feel safe to do so because your dance partner is providing a safe place in which your soul knows it can fly—for now anyway.

And then the first toe gets stepped on. One or the other dance partner makes the first move to present a need to heal an old wound that more often than not has little or nothing at all to do with you—it just seems that way. This wound might come in the form of jealousy, insecurity, or it could be as seemingly simple as displaying impatience at the sight of your wet toothbrush left on the bathroom sink. Regardless of what their issue seems to be, suddenly that perfect soul-mate just lost a few points on the "perfect soul mate scoreboard."

If only we are able to recognize our new soul mate is simply taking a turn at sharing his or her past wounds to discover if the two of you will dance and heal together in love or fear.

I have found that in that moment when he or she is being vulnerable and fearful, if I can remember I too will have my turn at presenting my sore spots, it becomes easier to remember compassion and the importance of working together without judgment, defensiveness and turmoil. I don't always win the battle, though with each opportunity to practice, I remember more often and more quickly.

My intimate relationships have helped me heal through some of the most ingrained negative self-sabotaging beliefs, and in fact we have managed to inflict a few new ones upon each other just in case we didn't already come in injured enough! But each one has served as my soul mate. Each day we travel closely beside another, we grow. We learn more about who we are in a most intimate relationship. We see how we struggle and where we feel frightened through the other's reflection. We watch ourselves soar, and we see what we want to *be* when we're with them. We can watch ourselves squirm as we also witness ourselves being who we do NOT want to be!

Romantic' partners are not our *only* soul mates. My daughter can be pretty handy with the button pushing herself sometimes! She is also a majestic lion-hearted creature who reminds me of the potential in every human being including myself. She is a wonderful mirror, reminding me of what I have yet to do with my life, as I watch her achieve in her own. I get to see myself as a mother of a striking young woman who blows my mind almost every day. And for the most part, it's pretty easy to love what I see in that mirror. And then sometimes; not so much. This no nonsense soul presses my boundary buttons perfectly because she has me wrapped around her elegant little fingers. She is so smooth, so sweet, too adorable! Her strong yet vulnerable nature is for me a powerful note to remember the importance of balancing the inner warrior while creating loving and safe relationships.

My son provides his very own unique soul mate services. No longer living at home, my son and I press one another's healing buttons in new ways now. He is a man, no longer my child, but my adult son. That comes with a whole new set of lessons and each one is a mystery and joy unfolding. At times I know I drive him absolutely to despair and to that I say…You're welcome son. Just doing my job!

Of course my mother is an excellent soul mate, as is my father, my sisters and the list goes on. We all have many opportunities to witness ourselves in close relationships and it is a fabulous spectator's sport! We can be hilarious at times!

PART THREE the dance of opportunity

As we seek that "perfect" relationship, we can forget we have many of them right here in front of us.

There are so many dissatisfied marriages, family relationships, partnerships and questions around what is right and wrong within any exchange where two or more people are involved. I often have clients ask me if I think they should put up with one thing or another. My answer is this:

You called it in. Only you can know what you have to learn from it and when the lesson is complete. And only you can decide how you want your life to look. Your response to any situation is creating your outcome. This is the time to refer back to being the witness rather than judge and jury. Every relationship allows us opportunity to know greater love and happiness if we choose to allow it to do so.

Abusive Relationships

Being a loving person and being a doormat are not one and the same. I'm the first to admit the boundary can at times seem very blurred when you choose to live in accordance with your spiritual nature. Abuse isn't always as obvious as being slapped or sexually assaulted. It can be very subtle and even when it is overt, if it occurs at the hand of someone we feel we are supposed to love regardless, a husband, parent and so on, it can cause internal confusion. First of all, be kind to yourself even when you think nobody else would understand. I get it! First hand.

As a sensitive soul who knows abuse myself, I can share with you one powerful universal law I hold close whenever I get confused by whether I should move away from a relationship because it's no longer serving either of us, or I should stay and grow from it.

That universal law is this;

Love and Fear are polar opposites.

Like two ends of one magnet

they can only be insatiably attracted

and uncontrollably pulled apart.

I have written a lot more about the opposite force of love and fear throughout this book and in *Permission to Practice*. I cover at length how we can become more aware of what this power looks like in our day to day lives; but I wanted to raise this specifically in relation to abusive relationship now because many people reaching out to know more love and happiness in their lives are at a relationship turning point and could very well be in a relationship which no longer serves.

So I will briefly list a few ways (there are many more) this universal law might play out in the day to day life of an abusive relationship. If they ring a bell, more lightning bolt moment will go off for you as you continue to read and practice. If you're living with any or all of these experiences in your life, please remember the kindest thing you can do for all of us is to know your full worth so you can share who you are with the rest of us! There is a world in need of your wonderful gifts.

Hints the relationship may no longer serve your soul purpose:

- You might witness a repetition of push and pull, love and fear, nurture and hurtful actions, which do not improve with caring communication.

- There is no genuine attempt made by the other person to understand your feelings and to develop themselves through the learning you are doing together.

- You might hear the words, "I'm sorry" *often*, yet the words are followed by an excuse for hurtful words or actions (which are often a result of something they believe you are responsible for).

- The same problems might continue to exist and mention of getting help to resolve it is not accepted. Or the help you might get may not be followed through in action so a cycle continues.

- You may often be told the problems are because of you. You might even believe it to be true.

- You find yourself taking most of the responsibility for maintaining the relationship

While I absolutely believe there is love at the core of every living soul, sometimes their pain is so great and their wounds so deep that their behaviors become dangerous, painful to others, abusive and/or destructive. I do not suggest anyone should have to endure an abusive relationship, putting yourself or anyone else at risk. Quite the contrary.

While soul mates will most certainly press our buttons from time to time, be aware of the buttons that are particularly painful, like a willingness to accept physical, mental, emotional or sexual abuse. Remaining in this kind of relationship is dangerous and unhealthy, rarely a place in which you might be able to establish a mutually responsible or safe place in which to grow.

It is my intention to write another book and course on this very topic as I find it is one of the most confusing issues to deal with when it comes to learning how to live with less judgment and more unconditional love in our lives. What is the difference between being judgmental and discerning in challenging relationships?

For now this is as much as I'm going to cover on the specifics of abusive or dead end relationships. Having said that, now that this seed is planted, if you are feeling this is speaking to you, please proceed from here with the knowledge **even the most loving soul must put their own need for growth above all else**. There are times when a relationship no longer serves you or anyone else around you so moving on is the best thing you can do for everyone. A soul mate who comes wrapped up in the form of an abusive relationship can be the gift that teaches you this powerful lesson.

How are You Responding to Your Soul Mates?

These wonderful button pressers come into our lives and just as they're doing a wonderful job of helping us see where we still have wound in need of love, what do we do but attack and defend! And until we understand the purpose of relationships, why wouldn't we? These wounds hurt! And they've been poked and prodded by someone who is supposed to love us. Until we become more aware of ourselves, our wounds more often than not express themselves as anger, frustration, control, hate, resentment, jealously and/or any one of the many energy-draining emotions imaginable.

Each situation in our lives can be experienced with love or with fear. As we explored earlier, we know we are attracting, through our natural energy, all people and every situation into our lives so we can continue to move more and more towards love. We've been doing this ever since we traveled as one cell inside our mother's body, attracting all that we needed to become two, three and four cells, until we became a fetus with a beating heart, and then finally a child ready to meet the world. We naturally know how to attract and create all that we need so as to experience all that we choose in this lifetime.

At every given moment, we choose *subconsciously* how our lives will be experienced. It makes sense we would choose to experience through a gentle loving process wouldn't it? Although, it is most often our subconscious mind not our conscious mind that makes most of the decisions. Our subconscious mind is filled with past memories that tell us if a situation will be experienced with fear or with joy.

When somebody says or does something you don't feel is appropriate for you at that time, you *can* choose consciously to be loving to both yourself and to that person—even if it means lovingly allowing them to leave your life. Sometimes people no longer serve a purpose in our movement toward our Highest Self, and therefore we can choose to lovingly guide them away from our lives. That's okay! They have served their soul mate duties for now and have other places to be. You can be sure if they are not serving a purpose in your life anymore, you also are not serving theirs. Sometimes the most loving thing we can do is let people go! Our soul mates are our greatest gift of awakening if only we choose to see them through our soul instead of our judgment and our fear.

If you want to look further into who your own soul mates are, take some time now and over the next few days to have a look around your friendships, your family and the people you deal with day-to-day you suspect might be in your life to provide you with some life-altering lessons.

You might also like to try the following exercises from your journal:

Ex 11b   **Opportunity to Observe Automatic Responses**

Ex 11c   **What Presses Your Buttons?**

Refer to "Love and Fear in Action" on page 126

See if you can note how you act out of love with your soul mates and how you act out of fear.

Finding True Love in the Universal Puzzle

Does it ever occur to you most people will say they want to know 'true love' in their lives. Some will say they have it. Some will say they don't. But most people will say they want to experience true love at some point in their lives right? But what is it? What is True Love? What does it look like in action. And can we receive true love if we don't love ourselves? Can we even give true love if we don't love ourselves?

One day during a seminar I was presenting at, someone asked me a wonderful question that to this day helps me explain the power and importance of self-acceptance and self-love. She said, "Why is it said we have to love ourselves before we can love another? Is that statement really true? I actually think I love others more than I love myself!" Suddenly this vision of a huge circle came to me. It was a jigsaw puzzle that looked like a map of the universe. I heard my own explanation as if I too were unveiling it for the first time.

Imagine the entire universe as one enormous spherical jigsaw puzzle, each tiny piece making up the whole. You and I each contribute one very important part of this beautiful universal picture, because without us, there would be two holes where we should be! Each piece of the puzzle is a unique shape and in any moment that we are living in accordance with our spirit, we become that perfect shape. However, as we live in fear, believing we are less than what we actually are, we become smaller and the piece no longer fits, affecting the shape of all the other pieces in the puzzle.

When we live life in the fullness of our natural shape, not shriveled in self-denial or self-doubt, we fit. We fit perfectly. We aren't the same as the other pieces. If we're trying to be the same as, our shape will be wrong in order to fit into our unique space.

Because of the magnitude and magnificence of this picture (puzzle), in our current human state we are unable to grasp it in its entirety. Like going up in an airplane where suddenly miles and miles of a highway can look so obvious yet when we're on the ground traveling on it we're unable to see much of the road ahead at all. So we have to trust. (I know. Easier said than done at times, but that's the way it is sometimes.)

In order to fit in, we need only be ourselves. We were all designed perfectly to fit in, to do our part, to fill the gap in the picture that would otherwise be incomplete. It is only our own limited self-image that tells us otherwise.

If ever I hear my own internal or external ego voice, disregard or abandon myself, I consciously remind myself I am a perfectly designed piece of a puzzle that I need not understand, but which asks only of me that I embrace myself for *all* that I am—the meek, the strong, the courageous, the loving and the fearful; for everything has its purpose and I need only acknowledge this truth.

When I am not being loving to myself, I am less able to be loving to others. True love must come from within.

This internal rather than external search for love means we cannot fail in our search. It is in this place of freedom we are able to love without a need to be in some way filled or completed. This is true love. And we can find it any day of the week if we're looking in the right place. Inside.

And the good news is...

> *The more we fill out our natural loving, unlimited, powerful space in the Universal Puzzle, the more attractive we become to others doing the same!*

And there's one more thing I should probably tell you...

> *The more we shrivel, dislike ourselves, judge, hate, reach out for co-dependent relationships, and so on, the more attractive we become to others doing the same!*

Oh dear. Maybe I should remove the last exclamation mark.
Did I make that last part sound like fun?

PART THREE the dance of opportunity

> **We can only and always love another
> to the extent we allow ourselves
> to know love.**
>
> **We cannot love without need
> until the need does not exist**
>
> **for we are always, all that we are!**

An unexamined life is Not worth living

– Socrates

PART THREE the dance of opportunity

So why not dance?

Why doesn't everyone simply embrace *The Dance of Opportunity* rather than stepping on countless toes and repeating the same theme over and over?

Why wouldn't everyone in the world choose to enjoy the feeling of gratitude for the lessons another has provided them over bitterness, resentment, and/or closing down to the possibilities in all of our relationships?

It works. It makes life more fun, fulfilling and exciting. It seems logical we would all benefit from such a choice. So what's our problem?

There is only one thing that keeps us from knowing all that is possible in our lives and that one thing is *fear*. It manifests in a multitude of tricky ways that are easily overlooked, tempting to pretend away, get fooled by, or chosen to ignore. Some of the ego's tricks to keep us in fear are quite clever! Cheeky. Funny even!

Become very aware of the multitude of ways your ego keeps you stuck in fear. Not all are obvious at first but the more aware you become, the more obvious and ridiculous the ego games become. It's actually a lot of fun opening up to fear once you decide to do it. You realize there really is "nothing to fear but fear itself"!

1. FEAR OF THE UNKNOWN

To learn and grow from any painful or challenging situation, first we tend to find the ability to overcome our fear which might present itself in the form of anger, anxiety, guilt, resentment, intimidation, hurt or a wide spectrum of other immobilizing or so-called negative emotions. We also connect with the part of ourselves that has the courage and knowledge to strive to be all that we naturally are.

2. FEAR OF VULNERABILITY

Growing up and discovering who we really are most certainly requires that we become vulnerable, honest and open to the deepest part of ourselves in order that we come to know our true and authentic self. We are taught from a very young age an attribute such as vulnerability, while in truth is the most empowering road to freedom, will most certainly cause us pain. We run from self-awakening because we have no idea how or where it might hurt.

It is said that more people are afraid of public speaking than they are of death. To share who we are leaves us open to consequence, comment and possible ridicule. The extent to which this is a concern will be directly related to how one feels about themselves.

On this road to knowing greater joy, love and happiness, we firstly discover our need to become completely open to ourselves. This can be a little more challenging that one might think! Have you ever heard the saying, "They are their own worst enemy"? Have you ever said it yourself? Have you ever said it about yourself or has anyone said it in reference to you? Trusting an enemy with your vulnerable self is not only hard to do, it is actually unwise! We will not release our fear of vulnerability until we gradually become our own best friend. I can strongly recommend it!

3. IGNORANCE

Most people on earth right now know little about unconditional love, the power it holds and what it means to be in *true* love with our own essence. I feel confident I can make that statement without any additional editing. I base it on the state we are in. We have little knowledge about what it looks like and feels like to become truly authentic. In our authenticity we uncover our true source of power; however, most of us have little knowledge about how to get from *here* to *there* in a practical sense. I mentioned earlier I have had more people than I can count look at me completely blank faced as I suggested they needed to embrace a deeper connection with self-love. The idea in itself resonates with most of us, but the *how to* is one of the things that hold many people back. Very few of us were taught, so why should we be tough on ourselves for wherever we are right now? When we know better, we do better.

In addition to not knowing better, most people are trained to believe that self love is selfish. Nothing could be further from the truth! Each individual is made up of a multitude of unique gifts—gifts that are part of our perfect design and handed to us without condition. Our job is merely to accept, be aware of, embrace and share as much of who we are as we can unveil.

When I looked at who I am from that perspective, it allowed me to see that denying my gifts didn't make me more humble, it made me limited, blind and unappreciative of what I have been blessed with! Who am I to keep my gifts hidden from the world!?

> **Knowing is not the same as thinking something to be true.**
>
> **Knowing is a result of having danced the dance so that now you walk the talk.**

PART THREE the dance of opportunity

4. FEAR OF THE DARK

It takes bravery and real courage, to acknowledge the parts of ourselves we consider to be "bad". But at times there are no other ways to enjoy the fullness of life's amazing rhythm without dancing through the steps that move us to emotions we are less comfortable with. Gradually as we choose to dance in love, gratitude and self-acceptance, these so called negative emotions don't seem negative after all. It need not be as painful as we often make it in our imagination.

Giving ourselves permission to feel without placing conditions on our emotions is important to knowing and loving who we are as complete beings.

5. PRIDE

For many people it is simply their pride that will limit them from discovering the lessons within a dance as they struggle to move in synch with the opportunity rather than against it. Many suffer from the need to be right rather than awake!

6. RESISTANCE

Similar to the issue of pride, it is often a temptation to work against the opportunity our dance partner provides rather than moving in sync with it.

I saw Richard Gere one day in an interview with Oprah and they were discussing the process of growing spiritually and personally. He was promoting his movie *Shall We Dance* and he was discussing how he was taught to dance for the movie. He said he learned that:

"When you dance you must be connected, literally. You get so close that with a good dance partner, you end up not being able to tell where one begins and the other one ends, who's leading and who's following." Then he added, "Just like in a good relationship."

As we become focused on the dance we are doing together, choosing to embrace the lessons, losing all need to lead or follow, no need to be *right* but rather simply to become more because we are united, we create space to know who we are and what we're capable of. We must work with rather than against our dance partner in order that the experience is all it can be. This might mean learning to dance a mile in their shoes, see things out of someone else's eyes, or it could mean learning a lesson in tough love. Regardless of the specific lesson, remember we are united in the experience, like it or not! As we choose to find a way to move together (even if our dance partner does not choose to do the same), we will gain the optimum from the dance and we will learn our lesson at the only level the universe responds to—our core.

7. CHANGE = THE UNKNOWN = FEAR

Another reason for staying stuck is fear of change. While the old ways may not work for us anymore, at least we are familiar with them.

In the same interview with Richard Gere, Oprah later displayed a picture of a very young Richard on the larger-than-life screen behind him. She asked him, "If you could speak to this guy up on the screen and tell him what you know now, what advice would you give him?" He turned his head to observe the massive version of himself, smiled that Richard Gere smile (bless him!) and said:

"That guy? You couldn't tell that guy anything! But if he actually wanted to listen to some advice, I'd just tell him to hang in. No matter what you're going through, eventually you come to know that all things, be they good or bad, will change. Change! Change! Change! And if you keep your eyes on the game, it just gets better and better."

Yes, I do believe it does just get better and better, but it is the part about *keeping our eye on the game* that most people struggle with. Partially because often we are unsure as to how to make the next play, and partly because we fear what might happen as a result of that play.

I am keenly aware that the process of letting go of comfortable old patterns and beliefs, albeit that they may no longer serve us, is usually a relatively frightening experience for most people.

Change will always create some level of stress. Fear of the unknown is our challenge.

Stress tells us that we are afraid, and when we examine the fear it tells us what it is we are afraid of. It is usually responsible for the blocking of our success and our freedom in one way or another. These blockages are the places within us that need to be heard. They are the places within us that store our emotional and cellular memory and our old childhood hurts.

Brandon Bays has an excellent book out called *The Journey* in which she addresses in great detail the *how to* of releasing our cellular memory and provides a practical step-by-step process to finding the powerful and insightful messages that hide within our precious emotions.

PART THREE the dance of opportunity

8. LOSS OF THE DANCE PARTNER = PAIN

Some people choose to stay stuck in order that they hold onto their current dance partner. Remember that a partner not only represents people, but also situations, jobs, homes, pets, cars, anything and all things that we are in relationship with. People fear the loss of something or someone who, while it might be the very thing blocking them from knowing greater love rather than supporting their awakening, they perceive can provide them with security in one form or another.

It is therefore quite understandable why it might be a frightening challenge to move forward at times. It is all well and good to give quick spiritual advice like possibly telling someone that the loss of their husband is in fact a gift to allow them to move forward, cull, and make room for greater things. While this might all be valid information, they might have just lost the person they believed they were going to grow old with. No matter how far down the spiritual path, for most of us that loss would *be felt* at some level—at least temporarily!

I had to laugh when I read *The Journey*—the author Brandon Bays, in a similar set of circumstances said it took her a week to let go of the attachment to her husband who had left her for another woman. She cried, felt the pain, let the pain get as big as she needed it to be and then, she let it all go; wishing him and their mutual friend nothing but the best…in one week. They remain friends today. I love it!

The human psyche is geared up to fear nothing more than pain. It is part of our inherent survival mechanism. We will do more to avoid pain than we will to find pleasure.

9. THE JUST GET ON WITH IT SYNDROME

On the other side of those who want to hang onto the pain into eternity, there are many people who can tend to get a little hasty with the healing process. They feel compelled to *act as if* or rush into suddenly feeling fine because it is perceived this is what we are supposed to do. We can fall into the trap of knowing *intellectually* there is a wonderful and deep meaning for everything that happens to us and though it stings like hell, we should simply and quickly get the spiritual lesson and get on with it!

The truth is that everyone must deal with life in their own way. Often we are given the gracious gift of feeling nothing at all for a period of time, which is just as it should be! This is often misconstrued as the *I'm over it syndrome* but the feelings can hit like a ton of bricks later.

The first step in dealing more gently with loss and pain is allowing ourselves to be present in the numbness or the pain. I am convinced that numbness is the universe's way of saying, "It's okay. Just rest and deal with all of this later. When you are rested the messages will come through your feelings." Pretending we are fine because we think we should be is hardly supportive to authentic healing.

The second step is to allow ourselves to validate our emotions. Somewhere down the track (which could take a week or several years), the final step is to *let it go*. What a person who is consciously choosing to awaken to their truth has over one who chooses spiritual blindness, is the ability to make the choice as to just how *long he or she wants the pain to last,* and then lets it go with love and gratitude when finished with it.

So what happens once we have let go of our need to feel pain? What lies after the pain that has become our very familiar friend? Who are we without the drama? Many people identify themselves as the drama they live in. Without the story of the husband that doesn't give them what they need, or the Cinderella syndrome, or whatever drama they believe they are stuck in, they have no idea who they are or how to behave.

Embracing the new requires trust both in ourselves and in a higher order of things. It requires that we let go in order to reach higher, and higher...

If you would like to read more and possibly play with this concept of being real with your loss and grief—look at the following:

Ex 1a   **Recreating Your Story**

Ex 6b-c   **Nurturing the Sore Spots, Finding Love Naturally**

PART THREE the dance of opportunity

10. THE INNER VICTIM

We are victims of our own limited beliefs.

I have decided to give the final reason for choosing not to awaken to our true-self a space of its own, because it is by far one of the most silent killers of forward positive movement. It is sneaky and destructive. Most people get drawn in to this trick somewhere in their lives and yet few recognize they are dancing in the shoes of the victim.

> **Victim:** *to be a casualty, fatality, the injured party, the martyr, the sacrifice, the scapegoat or sufferer. To be duped, easy prey, the fall guy. The innocent. The sitting target.*

I don't know about you but I'm not willing to be limited by any of these labels when I can avoid it! I am not willing to sit still and allow myself to be the injured party in my own life when I know how to be the creator of it. Why would I create myself as the martyr or the sacrifice? Yet we can all tend to do it to varying degrees.

> Being a victim happens in any moment you forget you are in complete control of everything you see in front of you. Doesn't that put a different slant to the idea of playing the victim?
>
> We visit our inner victim many times over. The fact is we can all claim to know a victim, but rarely does anyone claim to be one! I have learned that our victim behavior is present in almost every day of our lives to greater and lesser degrees. The trick is to be aware so we can decide if the victim is who we want to be in any given moment.

Do you believe you have the ability to change the world? Your country? How about your neighborhood? Your family? Can you do anything to change your own personal experience of the world in which you live?

When we feel helpless, hopeless and unworthy, we are in a state of victim mentality.

There was a time when I struggled terribly with watching people play the victim (usually also experts in the art of the Guilt Trip), because I felt manipulated by them. I was in many relationships with people who played the victim brilliantly. No surprises there! The universe will provide as many opportunities as needed. Thank you very much. They drove me crazy! I watched as they took no responsibility for their lives. I would bite my tongue until inevitably I would explode in frustration.

As I continued to choose to become more and more honest with myself, I came to recognize that in every moment I was condemning these people for pressing my buttons they were in fact my perfect mirrors. I too was the victim, as I chose to be nice rather than honest. I believed it was *they* who were responsible for my frustration rather than acknowledging my own contribution to the situation. Once I recognized it was *me* who also chose to be a victim and then chose to do something different, the victim behavior no longer bothered me and/or these people left my life.

How is your Inner Victim playing with you?

> *Have a good look around your relationships and inside the intricate and fascinating web you have woven in your life. Be as honest as you can. How do you play the victim?*

1. Do you revert to a child when your parents are around and then blame them for it?

2. Do you wait until the children are driving you mad before discipline commences then blame the children for your frustration or blame your partner for a lack of parenting contribution?

3. Do you hesitate to tell your partner what you want emotionally, sexually, or generally within the relationship and then cast blame for your discontent?

4. Are you in any relationships that no longer serve you, and yet feel it is *the other person* who needs to change? (While some changes might serve that person also, you can only be responsible for yourself.) How are you doing that?

5. Are you in a job or situation where you are unhappy and yet do little to change it?

6. Do you regularly complain about things? If so, what?

7. Do you find yourself being judgmental of others or yourself?

8. Do you blame others for your own unhappiness in any way at all?

9. Do you hide your true feelings in case they upset someone else? (I'm not suggesting we need to express all of our feelings all of the time—and certainly not without regard for others. I am suggesting when we hide our feelings out of fear of consequence; we are living a victim's existence.)

10. Are you living your life as you genuinely want to live it?

PART THREE the dance of opportunity

It is important you make the effort to find specific examples for the above questions and start asking yourself other questions along these lines that feel appropriate to you. It is also useful to ask someone you trust to comment on these questions about you as well. You can only become empowered when you become aware of the ways in which your own voice of fear is limiting you.

We find our little victim in a multitude of places, hidden behind resentment, frustration, or the quiet peacekeeper that others might even admire…until it explodes!

Playing with our victim-self need not feel at all *bad*. In fact I have learned the more I laugh at myself and the often childish antics of my own inner victim, the more quickly and painlessly I'm able to let them go. When we truly grasp the idea the victim within is merely a voice of unmet need, we are able to embrace her or him with love and support. In this way we move forward with ease and joy.

If you would like to gain greater power over your ego by becoming aware of how your inner victim comes out to play, now is a good time to stop reading and get your favorite pen or pencil out. Answer the above questions and/or you can try the following exercises in your Practical Exercise Journal whenever you're ready:

Ex 4a-b	**Take Responsibility, Release Blame**
Ex 5a-d	**The Voices of Love and Fear**
Ex 6b-c	**Replacing Fear with Love**

As we become more aware of how we play the role of a victim, we become instantly empowered to create something different.

So these are some of the fears that keep us from dancing in our truth. They are the reasons to stay stuck and when we are immersed in them, they might seem extremely valid. However, at this point you have a decision to make. When you have established all of your reasons to stay exactly where you are, getting what you have always gotten, then it is time to decide if you are truly ready to get dressed up, don the dance shoes and start to move to the *Dance of Opportunity*.

Watch out for **Guilt...**
It still lurks in the rivers of De-Nile.

Don't get sucked into the undertow.

THE DANCE OF **OPPORTUNITY**

step by **STEP**

As i look at the world through

the Eyes of love

I see there is nothing to forgive...

Only opportunities to remove

My own limited judgement

PART THREE the dance of opportunity

Step 1 *take one step backward...*

Observe Without Judgment

The importance of standing away from any challenging situation to gain greater clarity is well documented, and yet it seems we often forget this very fundamental maneuver when we dance with a partner or situation that steps on our tender little toes! Not surprisingly, this is precisely when it is all the more important to move away, remove the emotion and gain some objectivity...but then who wants to hear that truth when it's easier and more in our conditioning to blame our dance partner for his or her *intentional* clumsiness?

What does it mean in practical terms to observe without judgment?

I have dedicated a large section to this idea in the *Permission to Practice Activity Journal,* revisiting it in many different exercises because most people find observing without judgment to be one of the most challenging concepts to apply on a day-to-day practical level. Our ability to achieve this concept of observing something without placing our limited judgment on it is vital to being able to resign to and use positively the experience on offer.

When a situation is causing us frustration, confusion, anger, limitation, or any other emotion that holds us back from joy, we are in some way seeing through the eyes of fear, and fear is the root of all judgment. It is important in the process of finding true love that we stand back and become aware of how the fear is manifesting in our actions and what the underlying drama is about. As we grow to understand that our actions are not conducive to a loving interaction, and are really only fear in action, we also realize they do not require judgment, they require understanding, compassion and love. This is not to say you should allow someone to intentionally step all over your feet time and time again and your only response is an effort to understand their motivation. It is also all right to excuse yourself from the dance—moving away and allowing the other person to do what they need to in order to reconnect to their own unlimited essence.

* If you feel you need support, give yourself permission to ask for it!

Equally, as we feel joy, peace, happiness, and excitement, we might be seeing through the eyes of love; however, even when we are feeling good feelings we can still be prone to judgment. In this case, we judge this situation or person who we believe is *making us feel good* as a thing that is good. If we believe that something is good when it makes us feel good and bad when it makes us feel bad, then we give away our power to any external source that comes along! In this we are dependent on the outside world to dictate how we're going to feel today based on whether it's a *good* day or a *bad* day. The reality we create is our own.

Truly seeing through the eyes of love means being able to see any situation as it is—simply an opportunity to observe, unfold, discover and make choices about how we want to experience ourselves and our world.

Identifying the fear that lies underneath a particular judgment, behavior or resistance can at times in itself eliminate the resistance and/or the behavior and almost always eliminates the need to judge it as good or bad. While this is not always the case, it is certainly powerful in changing how we view ourselves and all that we are in relationship with. When we can understand that any negative behavior is only based on fear, then choosing empathy over aggression becomes a much easier task.

This ability to find empathy certainly supports the process of becoming empowered to rid ourselves from our obsession with judgment and helps us embrace our more natural state of compassion.

Observing without judgment means observing with compassion, greater clarity and as Buddhism teaches, without attachment.

In my years of working with people to support healing, I have discovered one of the most challenging tasks I can give my clients is to send them home to observe themselves without judgment. It is like waving a red flag to a very angry bull! It is inevitable when we are asked not to do something, we will focus on what it is we're not meant to do! How do we learn not to judge ourselves when that's all we have learned to do? I was personally quite outstanding at focusing on what I was not meant to be focusing on! For this reason I ask my clients to first focus on the observation aspect of the assignment.

Secondly, as the inner voice of judgment and criticism pokes its head out to play, again, just observe.

PART THREE the dance of opportunity

Understanding the need for observation in place of judgment, and the difference between discernment and judgment is important in moving with grace as we dance in relationships. If you would like to learn more about this concept, two relevant exercises in the Practice Journal can be found here:

Ex 2a-e   **Observation vs. Discernment**
Ex 3   **Discernment vs. Judgment**

Step 2

*look down, look left,
look right, look inside*

Check Your Intention

If there is one rule I never forget it is that the universe is smarter than my ego or as I've recently heard it called "mini-me." It looks only for the truth, and that truth is found well past our intellect and deep inside each *intention* that motivates our thoughts and actions. We might try to be tricky with ourselves and pretend we have understood and resolved a particular lesson in life when in fact we have not, or we might think we're coming from love when our real motivation is fear. We might be able to talk the talk, but it is only when we are walking the walk that the universe knows we have truly received and processed the lesson. And we walk the walk each time we reach a greater level of knowing unconditional love. Until such time, we are still dancing with the partner who is stepping all over our stubborn and battered little toes and we dance the same damn dance over and over again!

By the way, intentions are a very personal thing. They are born from a person's love and fear buttons. It is dangerous to assume you know the core motivation of another person so it might be wise to focus on your own intentions rather than those of your dance partners.

Oh, I admit it is tempting at times, but unfortunately that temptation is just another trick of little mini-me. As long as you're busy being the analyst extraordinaire, you leave your own dance and waste energy trying to do the impossible...dance someone else's!

A dance will last only as long as the two share a purpose. If one partner decides to step back and observe without judgment, in other words, come from a place of love, and the other dance partner continues a dance of fear—causing or living in pain, resentment, anger, being a victim, etcetera—the dance itself will come to an end. This doesn't necessarily mean the entire relationship ends, though it will at least change form. Their energy is not attractive to one another in the exact same way because that particular lesson has been resolved by one and not by the other. By nature they are not doing the same dance.

Very often all it takes is for one dancer to choose a thought or act of love and the other feels safe to follow. A good negotiator demonstrates this movement extremely well. They have the ability to empathize and provide their dance partner with exactly what they need in order that they might feel safe enough to meet in the middle rather than feeling at risk and in need of defensiveness or opposition. On the other hand, one can choose a fearful motivation and find the other one follows—this is the foundation for every war that has been fought and every argument we've had in our lives.

It is mystical, magical and unexplainable, but I kid you not, it works every time. It never ceases to amaze me but I see it in my work with many people, and of course I am aware of it in my own life. Either the dancers dance to the same tune, be that love or fear, or the dance just simply ends. One way or another—the situation changes when it no longer serves all the people involved.

Now I can almost hear the screams of protest as I write these words because I found it particularly difficult to believe myself at first. Until I tested it; over and over and over again.

Every time I explain the power of the energetic attraction created by love and fear in a seminar or group, there is always the list of examples provided by participants where this theory does not apply. Stories such as these:

- "I'm coming from love but my husband just doesn't get it! I try and try to get him to awaken to his spiritual self but nothing works. It frustrates me but how come we're still together?"

- "I'm always the one who people call if they need a shoulder to cry on or they need some help with something, but when I'm down or in need, nobody is there. I still have them as friends but I think I'm coming from love and they're not. How does that work in relation to the love and fear dance?"

Short answer; check your intentions again!

Are you *really* coming to the situation completely free of fear? Looking at the first example where a woman is *trying* (and trying) to "get him to awaken" to his spiritual self; I have challenged countless women (including myself) on this one.

It is easy to believe that supporting the awakening of another human being is an act of love; is it not? It seems the *right* thing to do, and that could be true. There is nothing at all wrong with supporting another and I would say that is a gift in itself. However, our intention is everything: the need to help is very different from the desire to support.

There is nothing tricky about working out which intention we might be coming from. So many of us more analytical folk can become stuck in dissecting the details of a situation in order to best understand it to the fullest, when the answer to our intention is quite straightforward. Ask yourself this very simple question:

"AM I INVESTED IN THE OUTCOME?"

When I ask a client to dig further into their fixation with another person's growth, we inevitably unveil a deeper need to fix in order that the so-called "helper" might meet their own needs, needs that are based on fear.

Fears if confronted honestly might sound something like these examples:

- If only he would become more spiritually awakened then I would be free to explore my own vision to a higher level.

- If they become more connected to their loving essence then my world will be easier.

- If I help them, they will think I am a good person and thus I might feel better about myself.

- If I heal others I must be healed myself.

- I'm not enough just being me; I have to help so I am lovable.

It is incredibly easy to fall into this kind of mentality. We have had significantly more training in how to focus on others than how to focus in a healthy way on our own core needs.

The more time we spend focusing on what *they* need to change, the longer we stay stuck in the same place; disempowered to actually *be* that living example, because our own focus is in the wrong place.

So what are SOME OF THE POSSIBLE FEARS we might have around focusing on our own need to change?

- I'm not sure I am strong enough to peruse my own best life if my wife/husband/friend/lover doesn't come along for the ride with me.

- He or she might feel threatened and leave me if I become too strong.

- What if living my own best life takes me away from my partner?

- I'm not enough.

- It is selfish to focus on myself? People might not like me if I do.

- What if I change so much I no longer want to work at this job anymore? I will lose my security.

There are so many reasons we might need to fix or focus on others rather than focus on the only place we actually can make a difference—ourselves. From what I have seen, there is a little of Mr. or Ms. Fix-It in most of us. The difference between *wanting* to give based on our loving, nurturing nature and *needing* to give based on fear, is all found in our intention.

This is just one example of how the ego can trick us into believing we are acting out of love when in fact the intention is based on fear. As we learn to observe without judgment it is important to identify our real intention for any action so we might be able to acknowledge and therefore change any habits not serving our highest purpose.

Being *honest* with our intention helps us to quickly identify where we are coming from and enables us to move forward in the direction we choose at a core level.

In LOVE

- In love we acknowledge another's need to live life the way in which they choose to.

- We are able to walk beside others rather than having a need to lead or follow, encouraging their desires regardless of whether they mirror our own.

- In love we have no need to "fix" anything as we trust that all things are in perfect order. In love we see the love that is within another and accept the fear as their need for more love.

- In love we acknowledge our own part in any situation.

In FEAR

- In fear we need to fix in order to have our own needs met.

- In fear we try to control (consciously or energetically).

- In fear our focus is on the other person's flaws rather than ourselves and how we might be contributing to the situation.

- In fear we do not trust that the universe has everything in order.

Fear can be quite tricky in the way it appears in our lives. We easily relate emotions such as panic, anxiety or trauma with fear; nevertheless, when we hear words like anger, passion, defensiveness, or even conditional kindness it is not as easily associated with fear, though at times this is exactly what it is.

Following, you will see a list of ideas on what love and fear might actually look like in our day-to-day lives. If you want to further explore how they act out in your own life, begin to observe without judgment and start your own list. You might also like to try the following exercise in your *Journal*:

Ex 5a-d	**The Voices of Love and Fear**
Ex 6b	**Finding and nurturing the Sore Spots**

Love and FEAR in Action

Just prior to being introduced to *A Course in Miracles,* where my theory was confirmed for me, I was toying with the idea that there are two basic intentions from which we think, feel or act: these being love and fear. While there are many emotions we might experience such as anger, panic, joy, or passion, if we explore further we discover that all emotion can be brought back to these two core motivators.

What does love look like in action? **LOVE**	What does love look like in action? **FEAR**
Light/Spirit/Essence/True-Self/Core Nature	Shadow/Ego/Darkness/Illusion/Mini-Me
Acceptance	Needing to control
Self-responsibility	Blame
Non-judgment	Judgment
Listening to understand	Not listening
Speaking your truth—with love	Accusation
Trust	Action through force
Faith	Inability to believe
Hope	Hopelessness

PART THREE the dance of opportunity

Love ⬇   ## FEAR ⬇

What does love look like in action?
LOVE

Forgiveness, letting go, freedom

Empowerment—believing you create your own world in order to grow more in love

Viewing life, people and situations as opportunities—gifts—no matter what form they come in

Being gentle on your own spirit as you grow and learn more about love

Taking ownership of your decisions, thoughts, and outcomes

Knowing that you are loveable

What does love look like in action?
FEAR

Dislike, hate, jealousy, resentment

Victim beliefs: "It's your fault I'm angry" "It's your fault I feel hurt"

Need for approval—Doing something because you think you should not because you found a way to want to

Ridiculing yourself as you awaken to the world you have created—Being unreasonably tough on yourself: "I'm too…" or "I'm not enough"

Projecting outward what is coming from beliefs inside yourself

Inability to feel, give or receive love

as I take responsibility for

my own experience of life,

I become more empowered to...

PART THREE the dance of opportunity

CREATE

that which I

CHOOSE

Step 3

Stand and hold the position with your head held high...

Acknowledge what you have co-created

Once you have observed the situations you have created, the feelings you have, the people and situations that press your buttons, the moments you are fearful and when you find it easy to come from your true self; and when you have been honest with these intentions, simply stand tall and *acknowledge your contribution* to where your life is in that moment.

I have found it is so vitally important to resist the urge to *blame*—be it myself or others while also resisting the urge to take full credit for all the so called "good bits." We are always co-creating. We have had many helpers along the way to our perceived successes and perceived failures. Just observe.

Our task here is simply to acknowledge what it is that we have co-created. We are never creating alone. We always have a collaborator and usually many, regardless of whether we can see them or not. They may come in the form of a sunny day when we had a picnic planned or our co-creators could be on the other side of the world. We may never know. It took me a long time to understand that this is usually none of my concern and if my co-creators are meant to be seen, I will see them.

Acknowledgement is a Tool for Empowerment.

Blame is a Handicap.

We come into this world knowing there is no need for guilt and nothing to forgive. We don't feel remorse when we cry in the middle of the night, waking our poor sleep-deprived mother whose eyes are gradually getting puffier and whose red raw nipples are more cracked with each feed! Then gradually, through many life experiences, we come to believe that along with the rest of the human race, we are in some way bad, flawed, broken, in need of repair, need to be more, or less, better, thinner, more buxom, less giving, more careful, speak more (or in my case less!), be good, hide tears, be stronger, pretend to like it, pretend not to, and on and on and on...

PART THREE the dance of opportunity

The teachings of our parents and/or significant care providers play an enormous role in establishing our own beliefs about who we are. This is not to suggest we place *blame* on our parents, teachers, siblings and whoever else *we feel wronged us* in the past, and I do stress this point. As we discover true love, we also discover there is no such thing as good or bad, right or wrong. There are only opportunities to learn more about who we are.

By the time we are adults we can usually at least intellectually understand our parents were/are doing their best given their own life experiences. The task we have is to actually *know* this truth and set free the past and all that is in it so we are able to break the chain of inherited labels that limit our understanding of who we are.

Somewhere along the way we learn if we acknowledge that we got something wrong or something is our fault we will have to pay the price of our wrong doing. For this reason we learn to protect ourselves by proving our innocence and/or find someone else to blame.

If we choose to have more peace, love and joy in our life, then it will serve us to use experiences and all of our relationships as opportunities to learn rather than people and situations to blame. A need to blame on the other hand will allow us to stay stuck in the prison of our *victim* self.

This does not condone nor erase the impact someone else's behavior might have had upon you. In fact, viewing the world in this way; that is, to merely acknowledge a situation as a contributing factor for our current belief system, empowers us to better look at our own lives without guilt, blame, judgment, or shame. As we do this, we move forward in self-love. It allows us to own our true inner power and move forward, living an unlimited life, together with every dance partner we co-create. Choosing to embrace this truth only leads to a feeling of vast empowerment once we are removed from a need to judge and blame.

You can never be too aware of how you play the victim. Even if you've already done the exercises relating to your victim self, you might find her/him coming out to play in different ways today than when you last did the exercises. If you really want to get leverage on your ego, have another play with your victim, who is often your inner child. Be kind as you become aware. That's so important!:

Ex 1a-b   **Recreating Your Story**

Ex 6b   **Nurturing the Sore Spots**

Permission to Let Go can be downloaded from my website, www.gaylamaxwell.com **"Inner Child Meditation"**

Step 4

Face your partner...

take 100% responsibility (for your part!)

Taking responsibility is so wonderfully liberating! It is an obvious follow-on from standing tall and observing what you have created. Now you are in a ready position to own it, and thus do with it whatever you choose. That's freedom.

Most of us have been conditioned to believe if we take responsibility for something we are acknowledging we are to *blame*. As we said in Step 3, in the *Dance of Opportunity*, the word "blame" does not enter into it at all; in fact if I were in charge of writing the English language I think I would remove the word all together! How is it useful? Who *ever* wants to feel blamed for anything? Who *ever* feels more mobilized through blame? It is a word that sits firmly in the ego/fear side of the fence and is therefore limiting to our purpose of awakening. Yet by changing the word and the intention from blame to responsibility, it moves us from feeling bad, immobilized or afraid, to empowered having the *ability* to respond.

Very often we blame the messenger who challenged us rather than take responsibility for our part in the relationship, which is only to observe ourselves, not the messenger. We are responsible only for our own contribution to any interaction and yet most of us spend more time identifying what the other person got wrong than how we could learn and grow from the relationship.

You are also responsible for the joy, the happiness, the laughter and the lessons. Keep remembering to praise your courage, your effort and your successes, regardless of your perception of their significance.

Ex 4a-b **Take Responsibility—Release Blame**

PART THREE the dance of opportunity

when I choose to do

something different

I get **new** results

Step 5

take two steps forward...

do something different—heal the wounds

Here is where courage comes into play. At this point in the dance of awakening to our true self, we actually have to act upon our discoveries. If you have discovered your life is not all you would choose it to be because you have unconsciously created it that way, it is time to make a commitment, take two steps forward, and do something different.

Your actions thus far have created what you have now. If you want more of the same, continue doing what you are doing. If you want to create something different, you must do something different.

If you discovered you have been sabotaging your success and happiness by self-abuse, become more loving to yourself. If your form of sabotage is disconnecting from yourself and or others by busying yourself with work and or anything at all to avoid connection; find the courage to stop, to rest and to engage.

Do the opposite of whatever you have been doing, thinking, or believing that has in some way immobilized or sabotaged your movement toward your highest soul desires. Become mobile. Take action. Face the fear—focus on love.

It sounds simple in theory doesn't it? *Do something different. Take action.* This could easily be one of those classic quote boxes in any self-help book that gets highlighted in your book for you to dig your teeth into later...but later never comes. I have bookshelves full of such pretty colored highlighting. However, step number three in the *Dance of Opportunity* is vitally important to anything at all changing in your life. This is where the analyzing is put on hold and the action takes place. You have already observed and acknowledged what hasn't been working for you. Now you need to do what does work for you.

PART THREE the dance of opportunity

This is not to say you must make massive life altering changes that scare you back into immobilization! One tiny step at a time. That's how we dance One tiny step at a time.

Release the pain. Be compassionate as you do so.

For example: If you have discovered your inner voice of self-criticism and you have acknowledged it is a blockage, your first step in becoming more loving is to pat yourself on the back for every time you pick up on that abusive voice. It *is* that simple. In fact every step is simple if you take one at a time and be as present with it as you can. No judgment. Every time you hear yourself being self critical, instead of compounding the criticism with yet another chastising lecture, stop for a second and acknowledge that you actually *heard* the voice at all. Remember this voice has been abusing you for as long as your memory will take you back; what an achievement it is to begin consciously hearing it in order to challenge the messages.

As you acknowledge yourself for the small but critical step you have taken (e.g., noticing the internal negative voice), and you do something different (e.g., rewarding the positive by letting go or challenging the negative), you have just started a new message pathway in your brain that says, "It is safe to face the negative and abusive things I do to myself." Why would anyone want to face their negativity and self-hatred if they knew they were going to get yet another criticism for doing so? That merely compounds the problem. And that is what most people are doing to themselves as they try, with the best of intentions, to face their demons. No wonder self-analysis is perceived as hard work!

The process of undoing what you have learned from childhood until now is a gradual one, as was the process that got you to where you are this moment.

As you become more aware of the ways in which your negative voice limits your movement, you might choose to counteract these unreasonable messages (and you *will* discover how utterly ridiculous and untrue these negative messages are!)

For more suggestions on dealing with courage and taking the first step, you might consider the following exercises in the Journal:

Ex 9(all) **Creating the Changes You Desire**

Challenging the Ego Voice—Working with Truthful Repetitions

It might take a little time to undo some of the negative untruths I have learned about myself. **I am ready to commit to learning the truth about who I am and the many gifts I have to offer.**

Challenging the negative voice of fear/ego is yet another baby step in the dance that brings us closer to knowing our authentic, unlimited and loving soul. But, to be able to challenge, you must have a counter argument. For example, your ego might be telling you things like this:

Your butt looks huge! You know if you were slimmer you would be happy. Stop eating! Now! Look at yourself! You're fat! Nobody is going to find YOU attractive fatso!

What can you say to that? It sounds kind of ridiculous when you see it written on the page, but this, or messages very similar are the language of the ego. The lies can be about your body, your mind or your spirit, but regardless of the detail, it is dishing up this kind of nonsense (no sense), with great regularity. In fact, most people don't even notice how many times they mentally abuse and limit themselves in the space of an hour...unless of course you have already found a way to challenge your ego and put it back in its place!

So let's challenge it by using some opposing arguments that I call Truthful Repetitions.

In the Beginning—Changing My Own Inner Voices

I remember when I first started working with the concept of affirmative language. I was not convinced, to say the least that repeating something I didn't actually believe could in any way support my growth toward genuine honest self-love. How can a lie support the truth I thought?

I was reading one of the hundreds of self-help books I was addicted to purchasing and I clearly remember feeling frustrated with the author's conviction that affirmations can change your life. This was book number 789 in my own process of unveiling so I couldn't imagine something as simple as saying a few positive words were going to make a whole lot of difference.

I was told to stand in front of a mirror and commence dialogue. I was to tell myself I was, "beautiful and loveable exactly as I am."

Let me set the scene for you. I liked to think of myself as a completely sane, intelligent, and strong-minded (translation: pigheaded) woman who was not going to get sprung talking to herself—and certainly not whilst admiring her own reflection as this author had advised!

But I was desperate. I was ready to let go of the pain and frustration that was blocking my next phase of awakening and nobody was offering me any better suggestions at the time. So one day, there I sat, mirror in hand, feeling like a complete fool, praying that nobody would walk into my bedroom while I was having a little chat—*with me*.

The first thing I noticed in the reflection was this kind of yellowy green tinge around my mouth mixed with the black hairs that made me look a lot like Homer Simpson or Fred Flintstone. (The color on my television was going, so everyone was a little bit more jaundiced than they already appear; though I'm sure Homer isn't all that well to start with.) Then, I noticed the big bushy mono-brow that used to get plucked every other year on my birthday, whether the old brows needed it or not. (Now I don't bother at all.)

So far, I couldn't see the benefit of this process. There I was, looking in the mirror, talking to what looked like a cartoon character of the male gender and wondering when my self-esteem was going to miraculously improve. I even remember thinking "I actually thought I was kind of cute until I took a really close look!"

But I didn't give up. The pain of remaining blocked inside was worse than any process I was going to have to endure to come out the other side feeling more empowered (I hoped). I knew I needed to work on my faith. I needed to trust that a million readers couldn't all be wrong and my attraction to the book on the day I bought it must have had some purpose.

I knew I had to persist if I was going to give this idea of affirmation a true effort. I knew with all things spiritual, if I gave a grain of sand, I would receive an ocean in return. I believed it was just a matter of changing my focus from what's wrong with me to what's right with me and allowing myself the best possible opportunity to reach my goal of greater self-love. So I persevered.

The books all said to keep using the affirmations, even when you don't believe them. So there I sat, talking to a hairy-faced *man* that I used to think was a relatively attractive woman, about things that I didn't believe in the hope that one day I would believe them. For whatever reason, I persisted. If nothing else, I figured at least I now had a man to talk to who wouldn't want to discuss cycling when I was in the middle of tearfully pouring out my life story!

I decided I would continue to say nice things to the man in the mirror for one full week. I would give it seven days – every morning before I started the day, and every night before bed.

A Nasty Little Voice of Self-Destruction

Much to my surprise, some strange things started to happen by day three. I realized I was beginning to notice the little voice inside of me that reminded me of my every flaw. I had never noticed my negative self-talk to that extent before. In fact, I thought I had a pretty healthy inner dialogue.

I think most of the people in my world at the time would have said I was a self-confident individual with above average self-esteem. They all knew me as an extraverted bundle of unlimited energy with an insatiable passion for life. My nasty little voice of self-destruction would have argued this concept to the bitter end. In fact my own secret was that I knew I was in fact exceptional at kidding all of us! I was quietly very insecure, questioning my own ability.

When I looked in the mirror as I persevered with these affirmations, the first things I noticed were the physical flaws. This was quickly followed by, the inherited emotional flaws, that were painfully unpleasant to look at. I did not accept myself for the person I was at that moment as my affirmation suggested. I did not have an above average self-esteem and I certainly didn't feel lovable just as I am. They were all just words the author told me I should say.

The first amazing thing I learned was that I did not feel all the healthy things I could feel about myself and now I had a direction in which to start approaching my self doubt. I realized this because of the fight I had going on inside of my head. The argument went both ways. When I was in front of the mirror and actually saying the affirmations, the negative ego voice of self destruction would say things such as, "Who are you kidding? Why are you doing this? It will never work. You look ridiculous. And by the way, you have a green moustache…"

PART THREE the dance of opportunity

a *gentle* voice emerges!

The funny thing is, as I was living out my day, even in the very early stages of this new practice, I noticed that when somebody tried to put me down, or my negative voice started acting up, I began hearing my positive affirmations running around in my head. I could no longer allow my ego to run the whole show. It just didn't feel right to me any longer. I was beginning to remember the truth about myself and the amazing world around me and I would challenge the ego's negativity more and more as I became aware of myself as the spectator.

Within the seven-day trial, I had gone from believing I was a victim of my surrounds to suspecting I actually had some power over what was going on in my world. I was only suspecting at that stage, but seven days is hardly a lifetime! It took the previous thirty years to learn all the untruths that were blocking my soul's amazing offerings. I figured I had done pretty well to shift anything at all in the space of only one week.

After working with many hundreds of women who have related very similar stories, I now understand it was this gentle, step-by-step process of acknowledging the achievement of small goals that is vital to our feeling safe to move forward in our awakening.

We must place greater focus on our achievements turning all other outcomes into lessons about what does not produce the results we desire.

```
There is no such thing as failure.
```

Real Change Begins

Gradually, as I practiced observing the positive and negative voices in my head, my world began feeling less hostile and my interactions with people were more peaceful and enriching. The internal battle between the positive voice of love and negative voice of fear continued, and it still does at times. The only difference is now these voices go to battle much less often because it simply is not worth my ego's effort. I see no reason to believe in its lies.

Very soon I began writing my own affirmations. I liked the idea of working on the specific areas of negativity affecting me most at that time. As I became more and more aware of the conflict between my voice of fear and my new, more truthful voice of love, I began noticing much of the core of the negative talk was directed at telling myself I was unworthy. I wrote several affirmations to remind myself of my worth. Though I had a long way to go to actually believe them, I knew I was feeling a shift, and it seemed to be a positive one. There was no harm in continuing the experiment for another few weeks.

I started working with affirmations many years ago now. They come and go in my life as they feel more and less useful. I support others in writing and using affirmations and I do this because it really works. I have historically been one who struggles with persisting at things, particularly if they take some time before results can be seen. I'm talking stopwatch here, not years! If anyone knows how hard it is to keep going when something seems to be a waste of time that would be me. All I can say is, hang in there.

We are constantly working with affirmations regardless of whether we are aware of it or not… our conditioning determines what we are affirming in our minds every moment of every day. The person who creates their desired outcomes is one who takes control of their own thinking. Stay aware of your thoughts…they create your life.

If you feel uncomfortable doing truthful affirmations…do them anyway! It is only human to be more comfortable with what you know. The only way to move from faith to knowing is through experience. What many people experience is how to let their subconscious run their lives. If we want to make changes, we have to do something different.

Keep on telling yourself the loving truth. Find ways that work for you. I have included a number of affirmations in the Practical Exercise Journal, but if you don't want to use these, by all means write your own. Just make sure your affirmations really are the truth *for you*. You will recognize truth, because it is always a derivative of love.

As you choose to do something different, remember it might become a little uncomfortable at times. It will also provide amazing rewards that come in the form of great joy, a feeling of new beginnings, unlimited possibility and if you are like most of us, you will discover an excitement for life you probably have not enjoyed since childhood!

PART THREE the dance of opportunity

enjoy the process!

6 HINTS

– Creating sustainable change

1 **Celebrate the baby steps.** When a child falls down in the process of learning to walk, do you slap her, or applaud her exciting efforts? Why do we assume that learning any new skill should be less rewarded?

2 **Allow yourself and others to feel UNcomfortable with the positive changes.** Sometimes your changes will not be welcomed by friends, family and colleagues. They knew exactly how to deal with you before, and so did your little mini-me! As you become more self-empowered, you are asking yourself and others to dance a different dance and they might not be comfortable with that. This will be their own ego playing with them and not for you to be concerned with. You can only change yourself. Now they have to find new strategies. Change demands change – and they may not want to do that! You have found the courage to make some changes in your life; they may not be ready. Try to use these experiences for learning rather than judgment. It is a choice as to how much others affect how your feel.

3 **Love your efforts as much as your successes.** Life is a process, not a destination. If we keep waiting for the final outcome, we will literally be dead! The world already has enough miserable millionaires who missed the entire trip to the place they thought they wanted to be. Why not be a joyous millionaire?

PART THREE the dance of opportunity

4 **Slow down and feel the joy of each new experience!** Someone once gave me these three simple words, and I use them every day of my life. *"Enjoy the Journey."* I now understand these words if practiced provide me with everything I need to revel in the gift of joy. Joy is sometimes hidden but always found somewhere if we allow ourselves the experience. It is a choice to look for the up-side in any moment. Not always easy, sure. But the alternative is harder.

5 **Trust yourself.** Underneath any self-doubt, you *know* the truth about who you are. You are a loving being who just needs reminders every now and again. Dig inside yourself. You know better than anyone where you need a little more love. Just ask, be patient and trust the answers that come.

6 **Meditate.** If you are not already practicing some form of meditation or relaxation, then I strongly recommend you begin to do so. It is only as we are still that we can practice connection with the part of self that is our essence.

To explore meditation further, have a read of the piece on meditation found just before the Journal section in this book. It's called **'Simply Meditation'**. Or play with some of the exercises found on the **Permission to Let Go** downloads found on my website.

Example:

I am choosing to live in the moment and become more and more aware of how my ego is limiting unconditional love in my life.

OR

I am choosing to reward myself for the smallest of steps as I grow because I know that as I do, I am learning more about the loving person that I am by nature.

As I *open* my ♥ to

Greater awareness and less judgment,

My world expands

And I am *free* to explore

Myself and others more fully

Step 6 extend both hands...

Expand awareness of the offering

This step is a brief but important one. Open your heart to greater awareness. Once again we are observing and reflecting but this time we are becoming more awareness using our heart over and above our head. As we reach out to acknowledge how many pieces of the universal puzzle fell into perfect position in contribution to our further awakening, we receive. And it is nothing short of a moving experience.

Each time I become aware of how someone or something positively affected my getting closer to all that I naturally am, I am in awe. How magnificent is the design of things that two people, knowingly or unknowingly can touch one another in a way that ignites greater love in one or both and therefore adds love to the planet more greatly than we can understand?

How many times has a missed bus or a red light insured a life went on to old age when a millisecond could have changed that forever? Since the September 11 tragedy in New York, there have been many documented stories of how people who would normally have been in the World Trade Center were running late for work got stuck at kindergarten dropping children off or had to stop for petrol.

This step of the dance is the place in which we are drawn even closer to our source of love just by the act of choosing to extend our hands and reach out for the fullness of the offered opportunity to grow. As we ponder the vastness or the universal plan and the synchronicities offered, we cannot help but feel great appreciation for the magic that is the gift of life.

In the sixth dance step we reflect on where we were, where we are now and how our dance partner has affected our life in a way that urged us to move forward.

Gratitude

makes my day a **better** place

PART THREE the dance of opportunity

We come to this place by choice. There is no time line as to when this step occurs. It is neither at the beginning nor the end necessarily. It is most powerful if we apply the gratitude step throughout the entire dance!

One encouraging thing I can say about this step is that if your intention for being in a relationship with people or situations is genuinely to learn and grow in love from experiences (rather than becoming bitter or more convinced of victimhood) you will most certainly feel this moment of gratitude more often and more quickly. In fact for me, it is very often the case that as I am actually in the middle of nursing the blistered toes in my tattered dance shoes, enduring the struggle, I also feel the gratitude and the wisdom that is coming from the experience.

While gratitude is the final step in our dance of opportunity, it needn't be experienced only when you think you have learned the lessons. In fact just when you think you "get it," there is likely to be more, so stay tuned. We rarely know the magnitude of the purpose of any relationship we experience because we're not alone in the experience. We can only see what we see in our own experience, (and even this is limited by perception!) Others who are affected by the same relationship also experience their unique purpose for being in a relationship with you. That universal puzzle is one huge and creative item! So if we wait to really "get it," we are at risk of missing the pleasure of the small steps along the way. If we wait, we might just miss the magical gift of a sunrise or the red light that unbeknown to you, just saved your life.

try to feel fully *grateful* and **bad**
in the same instant... no can do!

One extremely windy day a few years back, I was driving home from taking my dog to the beach. I had been running workshops and working with clients at several locations at that time.

I was in a hurry to get back home to drop off the dog and get ready to go out again to present an evening workshop. As I drove home, the wind was blowing my car so strongly I had to pull the steering wheel hard in the opposite direction to counter the tendency to head straight into the ditch at the side of the road.

As I drove toward one of the consultation rooms I was working out of, suddenly an old man pulled out at five kilometers an hour (maybe a slight exaggeration but it was really slow!) in his 1960 something car. I slammed on my brakes and shared a profanity with my dog, who was now on the floor of the front seat I suspect wondering why I got the seat belt and he got the flying lesson.

Much to my frustration we proceeded to travel at a snail's pace, and for the first few seconds it took all my strength not to run up his rear end, intentionally! However, passing the shop where I did the readings provided the gentle kick up the butt I needed to remind myself to dig into the place where I find patience and compassion. This man obviously no longer had the fast reflexes I was still blessed with. I was also reminded I needed to trust I would get to my gig on time – and if it wasn't at the intended time, it would all work out perfectly anyway. It just seems to do that, do you notice that?

At that second a tree fell exactly between his car and mine. If I'd been traveling at normal speed, it is quite likely the tree would have hit my car with Benjamin (my dog) and myself in it. In that second I knew I was being cared for and needed a reminder of so many things, but what I took away most of all in that moment was to be grateful for the old man who slowed me down just enough to prevent me from being hurt or possibly killed. There are so many things I learned from that experience and therefore just as many opportunities to feel grateful. It really is a choice to focus on the opportunity or the struggle.

Gratitude is truly its own reward. When is it that we are able to feel truly grateful for something and also feel bad in the same second? It is impossible! It is like trying to sneeze with your eyes open. You might be able to do it if you really tried, but what for? When you are in a state of genuine gratitude, if only for a moment, it is only natural to feel good about yourself and the world you have created.

I have also discovered that gratitude, especially when shared with others, has a magic that attracts true love. Remember the law of attraction? Like attracts like. We call-in our mirror. As we immerse in the joy that comes along with sending gratitude off into the universe, we call in other energy that is vibrating at a like frequency, and the joy becomes intensified.

On that day I believe that I created the old man who potentially saved my life. Through my choice to dig-in and find the part of myself that knows patience, compassion and trust, all virtues based on an intention of knowing greater love, I was given not only what I asked for, but more.

It really is simple. I didn't say always easy. Just simple.

Relevant Practical Exercise Journal Activity:

Ex14d   **Walking Meditation – Gratitude in action**

A friendly reminder that you can never repeat these exercises too often! I do this one at least once each week

PART THREE the dance of opportunity

Intention, intention, intention!

I have covered intention many times in this book and will continue to do so because this is the piece of information often missed when we are confused about what is going on in our lives. It is my intention to provide you with as much opportunity as possible to access clarity and purpose. The only way we have these things is by understanding our intentions. We have only two. Love or fear.

I raise this topic of intention again here because most of us have been conditioned to pay lip service to the idea of gratitude and yet so rarely accept the gift of fully immersing in it.

Being truly grateful is a feeling like nothing else I know. When I'm feeling connected to gratitude, I am very often left incapable of finding the words to express it. I'm not sure if in the English language we have even created them. For me the words "thank you" seem to fall incredibly short. It never ceases to amaze me that every single moment I am breathing is an opportunity to connect to that sense of deep appreciation. Being grateful is not simply being polite. It is a state of being and it is a choice.

As we Look to see the Gift within every moment
And Listen to hear the truth

As we allow ourselves to be Touched by love
And reach into our own hearts to find true love

How can we live without knowing true gratitude?

It is a choice that resides in every moment.

PART **FOUR**

things i wish i knew BEFORE...

Some things just work… others not so much!

When it comes to achieving success in whatever endeavor we undertake, be it learning a new dance or inventing the light-bulb, there are certain universal laws that are always consistent and completely dependable—like them or not!

We can kick the walls and rant screams of injustice, yet the laws are the laws and if I have learned anything at all in this lifetime, it is that the laws of the universe possess the consistency of what I imagine might comprise the perfect parent and teacher of life.

I think I've been very clear about my love for a good shortcut though I have tended to find most of them by going the long way. If we got letters after our name for every time we found the longest way to learn our lessons, I would probably have the alphabet after my name all before the age of 25! Knowing some universal laws is yet another shortcut I want to share with you. Do I ever wish I knew these in my twenties!

I have no intention of claiming to be the expert. Nevertheless, I am very clear there are a few simple rules that never fail—regardless of the situation, the people or the story attached to any lesson.

The previous pages in this book have provided a snippet of what it is to embrace life as an opportunity. I have briefly shared with you some of the possible reasons why people may find the whole concept too difficult to embrace, while others of us choose to live and breathe in opportunity, though still falling down on our tired little butts sometimes.

We are always in a dance, and with many partners at a time; but feelings of being stuck, anxious, frustrated or even depressed are a direct result of not acknowledging the opportunity that these relationships represent. Sometimes the opportunity is simply to see we no longer need to dance with these people because they will repeatedly hurt us! Sometimes the lesson is about looking at how our behavior, thoughts or feelings are contributing to the situation.

In theory, the dance itself seems relatively simple. We take a few steps forward, a few steps back and in the meantime we just have to remember to be kind to ourselves. We can even fall down, lose the plot and take a break without any sign of punishment.

PART FOUR things i wish i knew before

We would be wise to own a healthy respect for the law of cause and effect:

We are **always creating**
What we give out we get back
Believe it or not...Like it or not
It works every time

The fact is that choosing to be in a loving relationship with ourselves and the world around us *is* actually pretty simple. And while I say it is simple, very few who travel this road to self-empowerment would actually say that it is always easy!

Just today a very close girlfriend of mine called me in frustration about one of her dance partners. She pleaded, "Why can't I be blind to what's going on in the world like most people? Why do I always have to dig in and find love?"

By now she knew the kind of answer she would get, but in her own effort to remember who she really is, she insisted on asking anyway. It was her turn to forget today.

"Why ask why? What's the point to the question? *Why* simply takes you into the past which often leads to a long analysis about your parents or your man or your boss or whomever, then leaving that nice gap for us to make some sensational excuses to justify our situation and voila! A Victim is Born! You choose to take responsibility for how you experience life... or you do not."

Some days I'm sure she wants to hang up on me. Some days I'd even like to be able to hang up on myself!

Sometimes we can only ask ourselves to hang in for another minute, but if you are reading this book, regardless of whether you agree with every word or not, you are already on your natural path of knowing yourself more lovingly because you are choosing to search.

"Laugh and the world laughs with you..."

In no way do I wish to make conscious discovery sound like a complete uphill battle. It certainly is not! It is filled with the magic of synchronicities and so called coincidences that at times come in so thick and fast, even to the most seasoned traveler, they feel undoubtedly mystical. Sometimes living a more conscious experience is just downright hilarious. Our egos tell us some pretty dumb stuff (well its true), and it gets more and more humorous the more aware of it we become!

We learn to laugh at ourselves at times when we previously would have been a puddle on the floor feeling like a fool or chastising ourselves for one perceived "imperfection" or another.

We find strength and courage we had no idea we possessed and gifts we thought were only for other people. Something unexplainable surfaces. We meet people in just the right moment and we learn to let them go with ease when and if the time is right.

Choose to find others who want to play as they learn. Life can be all too serious and it need not be. We learn to trust ourselves and the magnificent universe that works together with us; helping us to feel empowered, light hearted, safe and unlimited. It just gets better and better, easier and easier as we move with our own natural rhythm.

Remember to lighten up, laugh a lot and lighten the load.

As you choose you change the events of the world

The wounds of the parent become the scars of the child only because their wounds were, and possibly still remain, unhealed. We have a choice. We can take their scars, making them our wounds and pass them on to our children, or we can break the chain by taking responsibility for our own movement from limitation to freedom. This choice is *our own* healing. It is empowering and it is never too late. The choice to take 100% responsibility for how we are thinking, feeling and relating in any given moment is the key to releasing fear, constriction, and self doubt in our own lives.

As you choose to find empathy, forgiveness, and love not least of all for yourself, you become like the pebble in a pond. Things will change. Sometimes it takes a while to become aware of it, sometimes it is immediate, but either way, you can be sure the scars are healing and they will heal for more than just yourself.

*All emotion has purpose if our core intention is to **grow** through them*

Finding compassion and forgiveness can mean for a period of time you actually choose to feel angry, hurt, disappointed or sad. Being in a space of love does not mean we are not human. We will still feel the full spectrum of emotion. When freedom from our past is the real intention, it is important to accept feelings just as they are, feel them to the fullest, allow them to serve their purpose, and then let them go. Feeling these emotions is certainly not wrong and in fact sometimes feelings such as anger or hurt can be exactly what we need to move away from a situation that no longer serves us. The trick is to *use* these emotions to empower and move us toward greater self love and acceptance rather than to simply justify our right to feel this way. What a waste! If we do not watch our intention when painful emotions come up, they can quickly change from supporting our movement forward to keeping us stuck in a negative cycle.

Either Way You Make a Difference

Just as our loving and happy thoughts and feelings are a pebble in the pond…so we contribute to events through all of the emotions we do *not* want to feel. Hate, sorrow, anger, spite, resentment and being a victim also have a cause/effect reaction if we remain caught in these feelings.

Keep it moving! Emotions are a gage. They tell us how we're choosing to experience our life. So called "good" and "bad" things occur all around us all of the time. What we're doing is simply using the human experience for our soul's ultimate freedom. Emotion is not something to stay stuck in. All emotion affects more than just yourself.

Once a person has moved past wanting to be a victim to their environment, I think the next most common reason I hear for staying stuck in negativity is that most people really don't believe they have the power to make any difference.

The truth is, you make all the difference.

I have sent many clients off to explore a week of finding the gift in every situation possible. The following week we investigate what happened as a result of their shift in thinking. It is inevitable we will note a change in outcomes. It seems almost mystical. We tend to find apart from the obvious things you might expect, people responding to them more positively because they were putting out loving energy. Often the individual feels better about him or herself as a direct result of more empowered thinking. We also find things occur that are quite unexplainable. Job offers come out of the blue, new loving relationships happen, or money appears in the bank, which was owed from three years earlier.

For every client I have worked with there is a story of the unexplained. It's apparent to me that as we make a choice to think, feel and or behave in connection with the real power that is love, some kind of magic happens. If I didn't have so much proof I'd be a skeptic. We need only keep our eye on the game. Be aware. I often wonder why we choose to live any other way. It is vastly more magical than living in anger, resentment and fear.

Practice finding the power that is love and you will be amazed how your world changes. Your thoughts of love shift not only your own perspective, but also your outcomes. This is not to say that if you do something *nice* you will instantly get something *nice* back. You will certainly notice your need to be rewarded for your niceness gradually fades until it has no trace. Nice is nice... but power feels fantastic. As your need dissipates, ironically the rewards seem to come flying in! As you learn to accept, appreciate and enjoy each situation for what it naturally is—an opportunity to discover who you are in that situation or relationship—you realize how all is of service to your awakening and you are of service to all.

Marianne Williamson in her book *A Return to Love,* (based on *A Course in Miracles)* states this:

> *"Externally, the universe supports our physical survival. Photosynthesis in plants and plankton in the ocean produce the oxygen that we need in order to breathe. It is important to respect the laws that rule the physical universe because violation of these laws threatens our survival. When we pollute the oceans or destroy plant life, we are destroying our support system and so are destroying ourselves.*
>
> *Internally, the universe supports our survival as well—emotionally and psychologically. The internal equivalent to oxygen, what we need in order to survive, is love. Human relationships exist to produce love. When we pollute our relationships with unloving thoughts, or destroy or abort them with unloving attitudes, we are threatening our emotional survival.*
>
> *So the laws of the universe merely describe the way things are."*

The law of the universe waits for nothing and nobody. It seeks no approval nor has it a need to be accepted or understood. It just is. Whether we choose to respect it or not is quite immaterial to its truth. We can choose to live in the dark, pretending there is no natural order of things, or we can choose happiness—coming out of the darkness of ignorance based on fear and going with the flow. It not only makes life easier, it makes it the natural joy it was meant to be.

Be Aware of Your Thoughts!

We have had a look at the constant dialog going on in the busy mind. The voice of ego is tricky and it knows every way in which to sabotage your success. So allow yourself regular reminders. As you think, so shall you speak and act. Your inner dialog quickly becomes the words you say and the way you behave. Even if you are well trained in keeping your thoughts and words to yourself, your energy tells it all. You cannot fake this one. If you think it you will create it in some form or another. It is beyond our control...except to manage our thoughts!

Encourage supportive family and friends to help you and you can help them stay conscious of the ego's games. Remember the laughter. As you dance with your ego voice remember how ridiculous its lies are. Laugh at them. Laugh loud.

And then remember you are **more** than your ego's thoughts.

Our constant task is to pay attention to the voices, which create our actions and therefore dictate the outcomes in our lives. Often we are allowing the voice of fear to limit us from having all we really want in our lives. We do this quite unconsciously. By becoming conscious, we can make choices that serve us. By doing this without blame or judgment, regardless of what we discover our current state of operation is, we open the door to rapid healing.

Take the Easy Road

The Easy Road is the one that welcomes challenge
and embraces each one as the opportunity they are.

On the Easy Road forgiveness is simple,
until eventually there is nothing to forgive...

it just is

Laughter is abundant on the Easy Road

The Easy Road is a choice we make in any moment.

As we become more and more awakened to our true self, we discover some past and possibly still current habits that seem stupid, ignorant, mean, and even ridiculous. Try to let go of the labels. They will only serve to slow you down and make the road of discovery an unpleasant journey.

Emotion is used for its human purpose on the Easy Road. It is not judged but rather it is recognized as a navigation tool. It tells us when to stop and bask in the fresh air. It tells us when to speed up and move away from a situation quickly and when to navigate around obstacles on the Road or to drive through them with confidence.

Connection Starts From the Inside-Out

> **It is easy to get confused between non-attachment and disconnection in spiritual teaching.**
> *There is a simple difference.*

Being *attached* relates to a *need* for a certain person, place, or situation to bring a particular outcome in order for you to feel okay. We can only control our inner world, which we know directly affects our outer world.

Connection is quite different from attachment but easily intertwined and easily confused. Connection is natural. All things are connected. All people are connected. *Being* a part of that connection is natural. In connection we have no need for attachment because we already *know* we are connected. It just *is*.

During my time working in suicide prevention I discovered the importance of our awareness of connection. I saw people so disengaged from their own reality they could hardly see my face as I sat directly in front of them.

I remember asking one girl to focus on my face in order that I might help her reconnect to something physical, but she felt completely incapable of my request because she had worked hard to create the numbness that provided at least some relief from her emotional pain. Many people I dealt with had become so disconnected from our physical world it seemed they were able to see past me. It was like I didn't exist because they didn't believe in me. They didn't believe in life. Their only focus was death. As they believed in death, this would be all they could see in that moment and all that was real to them.

My task was to help them feel safe enough to reconnect, even if it was only long enough to move them from a state of complete unreality to being able to see my face in front of them. If I was asking *them* to reconnect, I knew that I must model connection. I gradually allowed myself to feel what they felt, to be part of who they are, to cry for their pain, while maintaining a keen focus on my main task, reconnection. There was no greater teaching than this to establish a oneness with another human being. I came to understand that it was quite possible to completely connect to another human being and yet not get lost in their pain or their story.

I learned that when a person becomes suicidal, a part of the brain stops producing the life sustaining chemicals that unites us to our ability to feel a sense of connection to self and our world. Simply put, the wires that send the message *the most natural thing in the world is to be present in your own life* become disengaged, and the will to live ceases. It is most often a gradual process of losing connection with their true-self.

Connection, I discovered, is the thing that keeps us here. It is our reason for living—to connect and experience is the gift of life. And yet, it requires taking daily risks. Each of us have places inside ourselves that we have chosen to turn away from, not face or disconnect from, believing that to face these places would put us at risk of pain. To some degree therefore, in any moment that we are coming from fear, we are all disconnected.

Not all disconnection is as obvious as the symptoms of depression or having thoughts of suicide. Ignoring the subtle messages from our Essential Self about our need for connection can be gradual, subtle and yet still affecting our ability to embrace life to the fullest.

In so many cases, simply through early awareness and intervention, many people can avoid getting to the point of depression and/or other serious illnesses, which can eventually manifest through prolonged self-neglect.

Some subtle examples of disconnection from our True-Self are:

- *Only doing things that will guarantee success—limiting opportunity*

- *Eating unhealthy foods that limit natural life flow*

- *Unresolved anger, frustration, and/or hatred*

- *Neglecting the body, mind and/or spirit*

- *Avoiding intimate relationships out of fear of being hurt*

- *Sabotaging intimacy just when the relationship is feeling "too good"*

- *Smoking*

- *Self abuse—mental, verbal and/or physical*

- *Self-rejection and/or self-denial*

- *Excessive alcohol use*

- *Taking recreational or addictive drugs*

- *Working too hard—ignoring stress symptoms*

- *Not exercising*

There are many ways in which we can disconnect from the natural requirements of our essence. At our core we know the importance of aligning ourselves with healthy food, meditation for a clear mind, a nurturing environment in which to grow and discover and a healthy body that provides us with the energy we need to continue the journey. Anything short of that is a form of disconnection from our rightful state of being and our natural passion for living wholly.

Journal activity relating to greater self-connection:

Ex 14a **Self-Acceptance Affirmation**

Ex 16b **Continual Writing**

"Candle Meditation" found at www.gaylamaxwell.com

The Greater Connection—Together We Make Up

The Body of Love

As we begin to unfold, ignite, and remove the veil that blinded us to our truth, we will discover and acknowledge the light within ourselves. You are a part of what makes up this amazing universe. You are part of the One Body of Love.

Imagine a large body and we are each one of the cells within it. If one cell is sick with disease (dis--ease), it gradually affects other cells within the body. The greatest gift we can give to another is to care for and strengthen ourselves so we might best contribute to the Whole Body.

We only need to look at the fear we experience on our planet in this moment. Observe the wars, the terrorism, murders, and the greed, the degradation of nature, the growing uncontrollable viruses and the lack of respect for our wildlife. All of this is based on each *cell* (individuals, religions, nationalities, and species) forgetting we are a part of the one body. As more and more cells become infected with fear, we end up with a society whose focus is on false security, reaching desperately outside for rescue when the only hope is in each cell finding the healing within itself. In this way we support the Whole Body's well-being.

If each cell takes responsibility for the care of itself, nurturing, honoring and respecting itself as an integral part of the Whole, it needs nothing and gives naturally and unconditionally.

This analogy does not suggest we are not meant to reach out to support one another. It is simply stating that if we were all to recognize our natural state of love, there would be no need for repair. It is not to suggest we do not need one another because we are naturally connected to one another. Each individual part is very much needed to provide a function that supports the Whole.

Unfortunately, we live in a society sick with fear, and we are spending most of our valuable energy on doing repair work, licking our own wounds and tending those who will not or eventually *cannot* look after themselves, trying to heal the sickness. In a loving body, we simply serve the function we came here to perform. That function will certainly bring joy to the individual and to the Whole Body. This is perfect harmony and it is Heaven on Earth!

As you play with the activities in your *Permission to Practice Activity Journal,* look within and find the part of yourself that knows your own contribution. See the amazing being you are naturally. As you do this, you give more to the world than any other act of kindness can produce.

If you should choose to continue with this conscious process of unveiling through the *Journal,* by practicing the dance steps in your daily life, by reading other material, studying yoga, or whatever way best supports your unique unfolding…I thank you. You contribute to the healthy repair of a wounded world, a world that is so intensely focused on the illusion of fear that collectively we make it our reality.

I have faith that jointly we can co-create a healthy Body of Love right here on earth as each one of us individually contributes to the awakening of our miraculous selves. The darkness on this planet is getting darker as the fear is building around the world. This only means to me that those of us choosing love over fear will shine even brighter than ever before.

Be kind to yourself and please…

enjoy the Ride!

Relax!

Take a load off! Meditate.

Bring your mind home. Let go. Relax. Just relax.

— Sogyal Rinpoche, *The Tibetan Book of Living and Dying*

Having been a very sensitive and highly conscious person since I was a small child, I wish I had discovered this little gem a long time before I did. Meditation. Who knew giving myself permission to relax and let the world go on without me could be so blissful? I'm sure it could have saved me a few painful relationships!

In the quiet space of meditation we find peace and enormous clarity. After a period of time practicing this kind of peace and experiencing the ease with which our decisions can be made, chaos just feels like the ridiculous option. What we don't know we can't change so it is as it was; however, I'm eternally grateful to some dear old musician mates I used to jam with who showed me this precious gift several years ago.

I believe it is quite futile to ask ourselves to observe our highest or purest true-self from the inside out without having grounding in one form of meditation or another. In our chaotic and fearful world, staying truthful and open to our true-self is a hard road without having at least some basic skills in going within and connecting to our natural state of peace. In fact as I re-edit this book some years later for the second edition I will add...I believe it is impossible.

There are many ways in which to reach inward and in my belief no right or wrong way to go about it; there is only that which works for you and that which does not.

Some tools you can use yourself for stilling the mind are:

- *yoga*
- *tai chi*
- *relaxation techniques*
- *breathing techniques*
- *spiritual dance*
- *prayer*
- *chanting*
- *sound vibration*
- *candle focus*
- *walking*

Regardless of which way we go about it, to know our true-self, it would make sense that we first need to locate where it resides! As small children we live naturally in accordance with our essence until such time as it is gradually trained out of us. To reconnect, it is essential in one way or another that we find our own way to still the mind and rediscover the quiet place of peace and wisdom that exists in each and every one of us.

Without this quiet practice we tend only to operate from the intellect, and being an analytical person myself, I can strongly recommend some time out from that long road to China! If we are to know our true-self, we all need to find the place within that is the *observer*, the part which knows that your natural state is peaceful.

Some of you might have done work in this area and to some it may be a new concept. If you are already practicing meditation this section may still provide another way of looking at the gift of stillness.

What is Meditation Practice?

There can be much mystery around meditation for those who do not practice it. For those who do, it is understood that meditation is quite simply the practice of letting go of the day-to-day thoughts, worries and actions that occupy our brain waves and allowing a simple relaxation process to replace this busyness. It allows our natural state of peace to be present and enjoyed. The cogs in our brain work overtime—most of the time quite unnecessarily and often to our detriment.

We all bring our mind home in a way that is unique to us.

While there are certainly more technical and more deeply spiritual explanations for the art of meditation than I have provided, the simple fact remains that if you practice any form of meditation on a regular basis, you will gain the benefit of gradually becoming more in control of your responses to the activities going on in and around you.

What does it mean to 'bring your mind home'? It means to come into a place of calm through the practice of stillness. *Bringing your mind home* is the practice of listening to your soul mind. In the deepest sense, it is to turn inward and rest in your natural state. Our natural state is peace of mind.

In the Tibetan Book of Living and Dying, Sogyal Rinpoche says,

> *"It is like pouring a handful of sand onto a flat surface and each grain settles of its own accord."*

Sand does not enter into a battle for first place or the best spot in the sun. Each grain just settles, as it will, knowing it sits in its right position.

Often *we* are battling for first place and the best spot in the sun, the best vantage point so we might be seen, and hopefully be loved. We might be trying to find the best spot in the shade, a place to hide and hopefully not be found at all. Meditation provides the open state of mind, body and spirit that acts as a funnel, allowing us to remember that everything is in perfect order if only we stop and allow ourselves to feel safe in the natural flow of life.

View from the Mountain Top

Being in a state of meditation does not necessarily require that we are sitting still on a mountaintop. In fact the ultimate life is one spent in meditation. As we grocery shop, go to work, play with our children, or sit at the red light, we have an opportunity to be completely present in the moment.

Though I must say, being a mountain girl myself, sitting on a mountaintop is certainly a nice way to get into it! Why not? But if the mountains are too far away or you are a born water person anyway, simply find your own unique place in the sun. You might love your bedroom when it is all decked out with candles. It might be a courtyard or the garage! Where you meditate is not important. What is important is that you honor that space. This is your time to be completely present with yourself and your inner wisdom.

```
If at first you don't succeed—
change your focus from
success to rest!
```

Many people, in fact most people, struggle with meditation when they first attempt it, or when they are out of *condition*. Time and practice is required. Repetition. For me, meditation practice is just like a fitness program. As I practice, the muscles get stronger. I notice when I am in good condition, I am able to sink into that beautiful place of peace in a millisecond. In these times I am able to stay more alert, more present with any interaction and certainly calmer regardless of the outside stimulus. Just like everyone else, if I neglect to partake in any of the many forms of meditative practices that have proven to keep my life in balance, I get a little *flabby*, losing the *meditation muscle tone* that I had built up. The details of my life drama become intensely important and I am less able to see past the chaos and into the calm.

Life is our mirror. When we neglect our true-self and the practices that help us stay connected, we are easily convinced of the untruth that says we are in some way unworthy, and that life is difficult. We create chaos and drama to confirm our perception.

Allow yourself to simply sit. Don't be afraid to get it wrong! The truth is you can't get it wrong anyway. There really is no such thing. You will simply get it *your way*.

You will experience your best efforts and, if you choose, you will enjoy your own unique process.

Just sit and breathe. I suggest to clients they take only five minutes a day for the first week and increase it gradually. If you can feel yourself thinking, that's great! It means you are aware of your thoughts, which allows you to control them. Allow the thought to come in, and as soon as you recognize the thought to be present, let it go.

Why Do We Struggle to Find the Time for Relaxation?

I believe there are essentially two core reasons that one might struggle to move into a place of peace and relaxation. From the outside, the answer seems obvious. Most people tell me they don't have enough time in the day, or they say they have a very active brain and it won't let them relax. There is a great deal more to be found beneath this need to be busy and it is our subconscious mind that holds the power to assist us or fight us all the way.

What Lies Underneath the Need to Be Busy?

Two factors lie beneath the need to be busy:

1. The human belief in the need for protection
2. Conditioning

The Need for Protection

We have been well trained to protect ourselves from life's perceived dangers. It is not only our environmental training—it is an inherent survival mechanism in all of mankind since the beginning of time. We believe we must avoid the pain of life and to do so, we must think, plan and worry our way through the entire process, rather than allow it to unfold naturally. We convince ourselves that if we think enough, we can control our environment. And when we control our environment, we are safe. To ask your brain to stop doing this, when it knows nothing else, is like asking ourselves to stop breathing!

The ego mind that previously has had unlimited reign over our thoughts, our emotions and our actions, feels threatened if the practice of meditation replaces fearful protective thinking, even just for a moment. It knows if we quiet our mind of all the busyness and we use our brain for its natural purpose (that is to know love in all that is) the ego and/or the fear attached to it will have to go. In meditation, we hand over our fear in all of its forms and we embrace peace, even if just for a moment.

In that moment, our fear quite literally dies. The ego struggles with that idea! Why would we find it natural to do something that requires a part of ourselves to die?

Fear has become an enormous driving force in our lives. It has guided us since we can remember. It was our most well known companion. It has guided us into drama after drama, and it has traveled every chaotic mile on the hard road right alongside us. It even tells us that without these dramas in our lives we wouldn't learn and we wouldn't become better people. In looking around at the world in which we reside, it would be easy to conclude there is at least a part within most of us that most certainly believes in the need for fear and chaos. And why wouldn't we? We have been receiving strong messages from family, media, and society, but most importantly, ourselves, since before we can remember.

The practice of meditation moves us away from our belief in the deceptive self and replaces it with the truth that is our *real* protection—authentic self-love.

It seems in our belief system we have mixed up exactly what it is we need protection from! We need not run from ourselves, but rather we must move gently away from that which limits our full potential. If we are to live in our natural state of peace, we must release our potential-limiting egos.

CONDITIONING = REPEAT, REPEAT, REPEAT!

We are practicing something every moment of every day. However, when we are unaware of our practice, it is our human tendency (through negative conditioning) to focus on thoughts, feelings and actions that will gain exactly what we *don't* want, rather than practicing that which is tried and proven to provide more joy than we ever consciously thought possible.

What are you practicing every day?

Whatever you focus on grows.

The first step to undoing our negative practices is to become conscious of them without judgment. Most of us, unless we spend our lives in meditation, have had a great deal more practice listening to the ego voice rather than the voice of our Inner Spirit. This becomes our conditioning.

Observe your environmental conditioning. We are told daily the world is a place to be frightened of. This does two key things: it tells us we are unsafe, thus stoking the need for protection fire, and it tells us we are not good enough, as we discover no matter what we do, we are unable to save ourselves.

Observe the messages from our well-meaning family and friends, our schools, the news, and our place of work. In fact, even the drive to work can confirm we're not good enough. I'm still trying to work out how that all-but-naked girl in the ice-cream billboard stays so cellulite-and fat-free despite eating all that chocolate! Why can't I do that? There is so much incoming information meeting the belief that in some way we are not good enough and must live in fear. We are given many reasons for the tendency to trust our ego voice over and above our voice of love and truth. The ego is given far more daily substantiation!

The *Permission to Practice Journal* provides a few ways in which you can challenge and play with this idea of conditioning through media. Relevant activities include these:

Ex 8a-g **You're not Normal, You're Unique**

Ex 9c **Opportunity to Focus on Media-Fear Conditioning**

PART FOUR things i wish i knew before

Practice... **Practice... Practice**

Any dancer can tell you they didn't start out looking as good on the stage as you might think they look now. They took a new step. By their standards they probably looked pretty ordinary doing it. And then they did it again and again and again and again...

Our brain is a simple yet amazingly complex tool. Not surprisingly we can use it either way, by creating a complex or simple life.

Allowing outside influence to dictate who we are makes us susceptible to the trappings of our fearful environment. However, as we retrain our brain, we become empowered to view each moment of every day as an amazing and ever unfolding series of opportunities.

Repetition is important in gaining the greatest benefits from meditation practice. Quite simply, the more we do it, the more we strengthen the pathways of our mind and our body in alignment with our spirit.

After several years of consistent practice, I am now very keenly aware that as I repeatedly access this place of my own truth, I am more able to see the rest of the world though a quiet mirror. Gradually as I practice stillness, my world is a very different and beautiful place. Having been one of the world's greatest skeptics myself, before I resigned to the practice of meditation (and I do say resigned because I was very resistant to letting go), I had little faith that something as simple as stillness could actually change the way in which I viewed the world, and myself within it. It really is that simple. It is only our ego that prevents this natural process to evolve in our day-to-day lives. Life itself becomes a meditation if we choose to use every moment as an opportunity to practice being present. As we learn to be at peace in any situation, we allow ourselves to live in our natural state.

*Why so much focus on the **practice** of meditation? as we become more aware of who we are most naturally, we come to know with great intimacy our heart's deepest desires and our purpose for living.*

There are so many more benefits to meditation than I have already included above, and I would not even attempt to provide what is essentially unique to each individual. One benefit of meditation I would like to comment on, though, is the *practice* of meditation. Throughout these pages you might have noticed I rarely approach the topic of meditation without using the word practice somewhere very close by. This is quite intentional.

Within the practice of meditation itself we discover its greatest magic. As with all things in life, the destination we set out to reach is rarely what we thought it would be. Sometimes it seems better, sometimes the outcome disappoints, but it is within the experiences themselves we are given so many opportunities. The same applies to meditation practice. As we let go of believing we must arrive at a destination, or we must feel a certain way, or gain certain wisdom, then we discover a quiet space to be. Just be. Not being anything to anyone; just being in bliss that silence has to offer.

> ***If you can breathe, you can meditate.***
> ***Don't let your ego convince you otherwise.***

Each of us will experience different things as we let go and connect to our true-self. That logically makes a great deal of sense given we are all made with our very unique offerings, likes, dislikes, sense of humor, etcetera. It is also true you will find your own unique way of relaxing into the state of true-self. Some people never sit in a typical meditation position looking like the famous Buddha himself. True meditation is found in any moment, any time, anywhere. We find it in soil in our backyard or as we feel each footstep on the ground below us. While our mind is open, free of the past or future, we are completely open to the moment, and in that way, we live the gift of each breath to its fullest. This is meditation. Relax, let go, be.

We get RESULTS from our small but consistent efforts!

Some years ago in the very early stages of my meditation practice I remember having the toughest time making myself simply focus on my breath. In fact, the most natural thing in the world, breathing, suddenly seemed to be an impossible task! I knew everything I had learned told me to just to do it anyway. Breathe. My heart felt like it was pounding out of my chest when I thought it was supposed to be feeling calmer. My head was filled with thoughts of the bills, the boyfriend, the

PART FOUR things i wish i knew before

job and whether or not my client's television ad went to air.

I made myself sit and practice breath work for five minutes each day. My eyes were open and I chose to focus on an object. It ranged from a candle to a tree or the dishes I was doing. The object or activity I was involved in was unimportant. I soon discovered that simple tasks were easier to practice with than trying to use the action of doing my income at the same time, although we *can* grow into that. I had no idea whether it was making a damn bit of difference, but I was promised by all the so called gurus, masters and wise folk of the worlds' gone by that if I kept doing it, I would eventually feel the results.

One day, a month or so down the meditation track, I began to hear the same six words running around and around in my head, day and night. I found myself wanting to whisper them, say them out loud and even sing them! I might be doing the dishes or driving my car or going off to sleep, and there they were; the same six words over and over. Finally, after several days I stopped to really acknowledge and feel these words:

the **truth** lies in the **silence**

relax, let go, be.

PART FOUR things i wish i knew before

Shhh..... ...can you hear it?

~truth~ *~truth~* *~truth~*

The truth lies in *the silence.* As I pondered these words I suddenly realized the smallest amount of my own effort was being rewarded. I had actually been provided with six beautiful words of wisdom (I was sure they were my first!) It was only weeks into my meditation practice and I had already begun to program my brain to allow enough space for my conscious mind to hear that which was very obvious to my soul. The words themselves seemed to be encouragement to keep going, telling me I was on the right track. I was clearly being shown even though I was unsure on a conscious level whether this breathing meditation was making a difference; it was certainly getting into the place within me that knows the truth about who I am.

I can confidently say I started my meditation practice at the top of the class of people who believe, *"I can't meditate. My brain is just too busy. I'm too busy!"* Don't fall for it!

Find the time. Create the time. When you're in the garden, at red lights or in your first few moments of waking, take a moment to stop your thoughts of past and present. Your life will change, and it will become your own.

If a question taunts, or confusion is present, **rest.**

Practice meditation in whatever way feels right for you.

Confusion is only a product of too much external noise

Clarity is found in the stillness within.

as you practice...

REMEMBER THE 8 *Secrets* OF A GREAT DANCE!

1. Love and Power

- Only one kind of love exists and it is without condition.
- Only one true power exists and that is love.
- Love is incapable of judgment.
- Our capacity to love and contribute to the world depends largely on our ability to receive, acknowledge, develop, appreciate and then share the many gifts that make us who we are. This too is our ultimate power.
- Love is a choice, an action, and a state of being.
- Need and love are opposites. There is great courage and shameless honesty required to face our own self-deception, which cleverly disguises our need and calls it love.
- Authentic self-love is our first responsibility—get that part down and we feel liberated, safe and grateful for any and all relationships.

2. Soul Purpose and Relationships

- All relationships provide the perfect opportunity to know ourselves in both love and fear.
- What benefits the highest self-interest of one, benefits the other. The lowest self-interest creates struggle.
- Relationships provide the perfect mirror in which we see both the light and the dark of ourselves.

3. We Attract the Perfect Dance Partners

- We attract every person and every situation into our lives in order to experience the fullness of who we are, and release the illusion of who we are not.
- The greater the attraction, the greater the lesson (not always accompanied by greater fun!)
- Whether the lessons are learned through love or fear depends on the dance partners we choose.
- We are never a victim to falling in love. Attraction is just that—attraction.
- What we do with attraction is a choice.
- Being loving in a relationship is not the same as being someone's doormat… emotionally OR physically. If we are in SELF love we will not allow that self to be abused in any way. Some relationships serve only to show us when to walk away!

4. Intention is Everything

- The universe works with intention over and above conscious thoughts or words.
- To know our intention, we must know our emotional body.
- The universe distinguishes between our intention of love or fear. We cannot trick universal law.

5. Cause and Effect

- What we give out we get back, multiplied to perfection, for the purpose of growing, learning and discovering more about unconditional love.

6. Motivation

- There are only two core motivators—love and fear. At all times we act out of one intention or the other. Never do the two dance together at the exact same instant.
- Laziness is an illusion based on not understanding how to use pleasure and pain to help move us forward.

7 Find the Truth Past the Fear

- In the times when we least desire the truth, that is when we need it most!

- When the lesson seems too hard and resilience is low, reach inward anyway. Resisting the temptation of finding a crutch in the external world, instead of finding the truth inside, can feel somewhat overwhelming at times. Sometimes we just need to do it anyway!

8 Connection

- If the load feels heavy and you want someone to remind you "This too shall pass", or you just want to share something magical…call a friend/coach/support person group/Internet community **whomever is traveling a similar journey.** Let them help you remember your light rather than helping them remember their dark. Refer to item #4!

- Connection is different than attachment.

PART FOUR things i wish i knew before

Permission to Speak Your *Peace...*

Connect

Some days the conscious road can feel quite isolated, like you are the only person in the world choosing conscious compassion, forgiveness, awakening and love.

And then there are days when the path can be so exciting and magical **you just want to scream at the top of your lungs...**

"You won't believe the good stuff that happened to me today!"

Connect. Find others.

We exist ...
and we're looking for you too!

For more information about how you can connect with others to share the Permission activities please log onto our website and we'll put you in touch with our Permission Community so you can share the dance. www.gaylamaxwell.com

so here's the thing...

Keep falling down and getting up...falling down and getting up with compassion and even greater strength, knowledge and wisdom...Keep falling down and getting up...falling down and getting up...falling down and getting up... with even greater strength, knowledge and wisdom...Keep down and getting up...falling down and getting up...falling down and getting up with even greater strength, knowledge and wisdom...falling down and getting up...falling down and getting up...falling down and getting up falling down and getting up...falling down and getting up...falling down and getting up...falling down and getting up falling down and getting up...falling down and getting up...falling down and getting up...**Keep falling down and getting up...falling down and getting up...falling down and getting up with even greater strength, knowledge and wisdom...**

Enjoy your **only one of its kind,**

funk, punk, house, belly, shakin' that groove thing, hip hop, freestyle, Latin,

African, waltz, jazz, ballet, funny folk **dance**

summary for quick reference…

1. Love and Fear are absolute opposites and cannot appear in the same instant

2. **Our only two core motivators are Love and Fear. We are acting out of one or the other in every moment.**

3. We have the power to choose how we feel, think and behave – and it serves us most powerfully when we practice in the most challenging situations.

4. **We are not victims to our surrounds unless we choose to perceive ourselves as victims.**

5. The kindest thing we can do for those around us is to be self-loving because when we are, we naturally need less and give more.

6. We were each created perfectly to fulfill our life purpose. Our task is to become acquainted with this unique self so we might realize our full potential.

7. We cannot change another through force. Love is the only real power we have. Anything else is temporary.

8. Choosing to be conscious, compassionate and non-judgmental allows us to feel more moments of deep joy.

9. Forgiveness starts with our ability to forgive ourselves.

10. Guilt keeps us stuck in the need to blame. It is the foundation of resistance to take responsibility and it makes forgiveness impossible.

11. Everyone does the best they can. Sometimes it works for us. Sometimes it doesn't. Always there is a lesson. It's okay to move away when someone or something no longer serves your highest purpose.

12. **How long a dance partner should be welcomed on our stage is completely up to us. If we choose to learn through ease and flow or through pain and frustration is completely up to us.**

13. Nobody knows your unique dance like you do.

14. **YOU are the advice, the love and the friendship you are looking for.**

15. Allowing others to treat us with disrespect or in any way less than what we desire and deserve is based on a fear not love.

Practice happiness

Practice peace

Practice love

Over **and over**

and over....

PART FIVE *permission to practice* activity journal

My wish for you, for me, for the world, is that we will give ourselves **Permission** *to be the peace on this earth we hunger for...*

One minute,

one thought,

one tiny gesture at a time.

Permission to Practice
It's Just Life

If you are not doing so already, your *Permission to Practice Activity Journal* is the next step in this dance…

As I said at the beginning of this book, reading is only the first part. In order to move with more love, joy, clarity and passion in your life, you must take action. Constant action.

The opportunities to practice love and happiness show up in every moment we breathe air.

That's the very truth most people tend to overlook. We can read all the pretty little inspirational books filled with powerful sayings; and take those extra five minutes to download the "inspirational" video clips showing up in our 'inboxes'. (You know the ones that have the perfect blend of music, imagery and emotive sayings about compassion, love, and the power we have to co-create, etcetera, etcetera…

And we can hope somehow the words might jump off the page and become true about our lives.

But here's the thing…

We can't Trick the Universe!

In every living moment we choose to grow in love or retract in fear.

The opportunities can be very subtle because we are not highly conditioned to view the things which challenge us as opportunities but rather we might see them to be problems. Opportunity wrapped in challenge can appear confusing because we are sold the need to defend ourselves, protect ourselves, blame the other guy, compare, and compete, and so on. And we are sold these 'norms' over love, every day of the week. So to grow in honest-self expression it requires conscious choice and the courage to choose our own convictions over what might be popular in any given moment.

The opportunities to practice happiness, love and peace in our lives can also come wrapped up in moments of pure bliss! These little gems most certainly provide balance, deep joy, rejuvenation, healing and they bring us a level of clarity we can know only know through practicing conscious living.

Regardless of how your opportunities to practice come knocking, I hope you will enjoy the magic... and spread it around.

Some help along the way...

- Use the *Permission to Practice Activity Journal* so you can experience rather than just read these concepts.

- Get a buddy, or many so you can play with these ideas together.

- Do one thing every day, regardless if it is just taking a deep breath with the intention of expanding love and happiness in your life.

- Give yourself Permission to know the kind of deep happiness that brings a smile to your face at times when you have no idea why...

> **Give yourself Permission to stuff up**, be **hilariously human,**
> *fall down and get back up with dignity*
> *and a little more wisdom*

practice *exposes* perfect...
The good news with all of this practicing is, as long as our intention is based on love, we can't stuff up! Somewhat more amazing to me is this; even when we are coming from fear and not remotely close to being all of the amazing things we are by nature, Love is still stronger and bigger than our fearful illusions so guess what? We still can't stuff up. We might get a little side tracked, but the universe has a way (an infinite number of them actually) of helping us out of our fear and back home to love and happiness. All we need do is one simple thing...practice love. As we do so, the perfection of each moment will be exposed.

How cool is that?

Imagine
all the people living life in

peace

— *John Lennon*

PART FIVE *permission to practice activity journal*

Truth is like the sun...you can shut it out for a time but it ain't going nowhere

- Elvis

"Heal the world, make it better place, for me and for you... and the entire human race"

– Michael Jackson

*Emancipate yourself from mental slavery
None but ourselves can free our minds*

– Bob Marley

Dying to be heard
When will we really listen?

Artwork by Ric Bennett: www.ricbennettartandmusic.com.au

Thanks for the Dance...

May we meet again!

This is the end of **one book.** This moment is just the beginning of the rest of your unique life! Keep dancing! Keep giving yourself *Permission* to be all that you can be.

Until we meet again, may the magic and the challenges inspire you to keep on dancing to your own unique rhythm.

Much love to you,

Gayla.

PART FIVE *permission to practice* activity journal

IF LIFE IS NOT A DRESS REHEARSAL...

HOW THEN DO WE EVER DISCOVER AND REFINE

OUR OWN UNIQUE OFFERING TO THE SHOW **?**

IT'S **ALL** BACKSTAGE TO ME!

About the Author

Gayla Maxwell was born in Canada and has made Australia her home since 1980.

As a qualified Clinical Hypnotist and Master Trainer in suicide prevention, Gayla provided training to psychologists, general practitioners, police, ambulance service, and all areas of the medical profession. During that time she became aware of the need to design *preventative programs*, focusing more on mental *fitness* and less on mental *illness.*

She went on to create and facilitate Cultural Change programs for such corporations as BMW, working with their top management teams, and marketing guru Simon Hammond brand.

As a singer/songwriter herself, Gayla now gives herself permission to use her knowledge in service to to her real passion, working with like-minded people in the creative industries. She has developed specialized programs for actors, musicians, writers and anyone wanting to gain full benefits from their creative minds - overcoming subconscious beliefs which limit ultimate success.

She is a well respected writer, a playful and inspirational speaker who teaches the mastery of emotional fitness.

At home you will probably find her hanging out with Bob the dog, ('Robert' when he gets on her bed with dirty paws) and a typically bossy cat called Bruce.

Thanks to my dear friends family and clients…

To Simone, Kim, Tony, Ian, Greg, Tane, Victoria and the rest of you wonderful souls who listened on a telephone as I 'processed out loud'. May your ears heal over well! To Paula, my editor, friend and sister, I thank you for filling in the missing pieces, (and we both know we're not just talking here now!) To Ric, I thank you for the the many lessons, and for always believing in the full possibility of *Permission*.

Thanks to my greatest teachers…

Nothing really stays the same. In my life that evolving door can seem like a spinning top at times! But when it comes to knowing I'm loved there are two people who remain solid and still in my ever evolving world, and these are my two children Dylan and Jessica.

Dylan, (forever my Big Baby Boy) – We're told laughter is the best medicine. You have certainly dished up more than a few lovin' spoonfuls on our shared travels. I thank you for the joy, the friendship, the lessons and the love.

You inspire me as I witness your profound compassion for family, friends and animals, (which are sometimes all one and the same in our family!)

I watch now, from here to there, as you step into the next wonderful phase of your life, dancing to a new song, learning brand new steps…and I too learn some more.

 Enjoy every moment…I feel so blessed for every one you share with me.

My beautiful daughter Jessica, who knows me like nobody else, and loves me anyway…

I thank you for your courage, your forgiveness, your undying loyalty, your wisdom and that deliciously infectious giggle! Did I mention your feistiness? Love it.

You inspire me with hope for a new world as I experience your remarkable understanding of universal order, (of course you'd have to use different words!) I am constantly reminded you are part of an insightful new generation of women… and the future rests in those elegant yet powerful hands. All is good in the world.

Dylan & Jess, You are the *why* and the *how* I wrote this book.

the beginning...

Lightning Source UK Ltd.
Milton Keynes UK
UKHW030925200721
387465UK00010B/1895